# CAN'T LET GO

# PART ONE

## THE TRIAL

## AND

## TRIBULATION

# CAN'T LET GO

# PART ONE

## THE TRIAL

## AND

## TRIBULATION

### BY CC FANN

Published by JABS PUBLICATIONS

Copyright by © 2006 by C C Fann

All rights reserved, which includes the right to reproduce this book or portions thereof in any form whatsoever except as provided by the U.S. Copyright law.

ISBN 1-59872-452-5

Text and Composition: Asta Publications, LLC

PUBLISHER'S NOTE

This book is a work of fiction. Names, characters, places, and incidents either are the product of the author's imagination or are used fictitiously, and any resemblance to actual persons, living or dead business establishments, events, or locales is entirely coincidental.

Without limiting the rights under copyright reserved above, no part of this publication may be reproduced, stored in or introduced into a retrieval system, or transmitted, in any form, or by any means(electronic, mechanical, photocopying, recording, or otherwise), without the prior written permission of both the copyright owner and the above publisher of this book.

The scanning, uploading, and distribution of this book via the Internet or via any other means without the permission of the publisher is illegal and punishable by law. Please purchase only authorized electronic editions, and do not participate in or encourage electronic piracy of copyright materials. Your support of the author's right is appreciated While the author's has made every effort to provide accurate telephone numbers and Internet addresses at the time of publication, neither the publisher nor the author assumes any responsibility for errors, or for changes that occur after publication. Further, the publisher does not have any control over and does not assume any responsibility for author or third-party Web sites or their content.

Printed in the United States of America

# Letter From The Author

First this is a fictional account-it was written to teach a lesson that God is not pleased when you date a married person. Mckenzie Scott is a character that was created to teach all of us about the dating game. This is the first of five relationships. Don't judge her because you might be her one day. Please enjoy and learn.

CC Fann

# Introduction

This book is for ordinary people. Before there was success, everyone had trials and tribulations. You even have them after success. Usually, you can hide it better with money. You lived among the crabs who claimed they had your best interest at heart.

You often hear you are living in the times of revelations. At least, the so called Christians and Christians would say. The So Called Christians who are sinning figured they have enough time before it happens. The Some Times They Are Christians with their righteous beliefs are wondering why the ones that are sinning are living the good life. But I was glad there was a group called The True Christians. Because, they don't worry about what someone else is doing. They believe in the Lord and he will take care of anything.

You have read many books about doctors, lawyers, and artists who in their own right have drama. Especially, when it hits the society page, it is real drama then. But what about the unknown professionals (the middle and lower class), we have day to day drama too. For us the drama is when it hits the telephone line. But I guess it is expected that we have our own drama too. In our life, it is drama just to pay the bills. This is one woman's story of living on a salary job, living from check to check, and trying to deal with all aspects of life. How she robbed, cheated, stole and bounced checks from Peter just to pay Paul. How she dealt with the ordeal of raising her children alone.

Is her faith, her upbringing, moral values and/or the love of her children enough to get her through? This book is for all faiths and non believers alike because it does not matter what you call your savior-we all have done wrong.

So this book will open your eyes no matter who you are, where you are, or how much you have -you will relate, whether you be a man or a woman. You will understand. You may not want to admit it or just don't want to talk about it, or maybe you are going through it right now.

You will say everyone has had a bad relationship, so what. But does everyone have a relationship that you know will not benefit you right from the start? The kind of relationship that for reasons that you believe are right you will compromise everything (faith, family and friends) for the lust of a man or a woman. A relationship you can't forget.

Then you will wake up (if you wake up) and you will wonder, was it all worth it? Was it worth what you went through?

God destroyed Sodom and Gomorrah for all types of sins. What price will you and I pay for our sins? My best friend Mona, who plays the mother role for the M-Connection, (Moria, Monica, Maxine, and me, McKenzie Scott), often gives us advice. We were all single mothers who have fought to get where we were. We all had different types of gifts that we could use to make other income. NO!-none us were prostitutes (that I knew about). Maxine, Mona and Moria could do taxes like no other. Monica can slam some braid and pin plaits. That is with or without weave. I could type any kind of documents (resumes, legal briefs, and church programs).

Not only does Mona play the mother role, she plays the preacher role, too. She would say a woman needs to for once fall in love with the Lord-the same way we fall in love with a man. We need to live with the Lord, work with the Lord and raise your children with the Lord. Then he will give us a companion that is deserving of us. We need to stop going from man to man.

So no matter what religion, race or social status you are, take this journey of one woman's life as she goes through good and bad times. Will she make it? Will she live happily ever after, or just live?

# Chapter 1

Ending a relationship, it's never good. Here I was 40, single with four children and only married once. Let me be short-my one and only prince I had been waiting for entered my life, or at least I thought he did. Eight months later, tragedy struck-he was paralyzed in an automobile accident. His name was Darius Howard. He was a correctional officer who was assigned to the special task unit for the Department of Corrections. But I was so in love that I was completely blind. Nothing mattered but him. All I wanted was to be with my man in every way possible. I just wanted to be there for him...

He wasn't divorced from his wife. But they were separated. He was living with his aunt, before the accident. We ended up pursuing a relationship. He divorced his wife. He said it was mutual. He said they didn't love each other anymore. We built a beautiful home together, which was handicapped accessible. Can you believe it? I moved out from my mother to the project, then to a single trailer that was a fire hazard, and now, my dream home.

The paralysis, for some reason, I did not have a problem dealing with. I guess that was love for you. Everything was perfect: we had a beautiful home with a 30 year mortgage and I was engaged with a $1000.00 ring on my finger. I encouraged him to attend college to finish up his degree, we both were working, we had a great sex life, and my children were happy. (I know you are wondering what kind of sex life).

Then it happened: we grew apart-we didn't talk anymore. Some miracle happens; he regains the use of his legs. He could walk again. When it came down to us talking about a date to get married-we could never agree. It was as if he was stalling. Then he finally said it-he wasn't ready for marriage. We had a terrible breakup. Financially things were not good. So we lost everything-that's enough on that-you need to read the next book, because that's where he really gets down with his undercover evil self.

# Chapter 2

See, I'm 5'3", nice brown skin, a combination of a Tony Braxton-Halle Berry haircut-a petite figure 36-26-34 with abs-no one can believe my age. So it wasn't hard in finding a man. It was just keeping him. That was hard. I used to have a policy to never date a man you work with; since I struck out with Howard I said I'd never do it again.

In my profession as a correctional officer, divorces, extra-marital affairs and infidelity must be a part of the job. In the job description it states any other duties assigned-you would think that's what it means. It's a hidden policy because you hardly get into trouble for it. The stupidest thing is you can look on the job announcement, estimate the year and determine how much someone makes. If they got kids-what kind of a car, credit cards, see what they have left. The question is what can or will they be able to do for you on their salary.

But I was an independent woman-I didn't want anyone taking care of me. I didn't want to be a voluntary slave. For those who don't know, let me define VOLUNTARY SLAVERY: He gives you money for your bills, hair dos and maybe a outfit from time to time, you perform great sex at his convenience, you are available at his beck and call-we don't do anything in public-you can't date another man or at least get caught doing it, and he needs a daily agenda. He also monitors who you can have as friends. Tell me that's not voluntary slavery.

Oh I forgot one clause-the one no one likes to talk about, depending on the brother. He might be special-you know-he thinks that loving someone means knocking the hell out of them. SHHH-be quiet, we can't say it too loud. We don't want anybody to know. That every now and again we wear permanent make-up. You know, darker eye shadow-bigger luscious lips probably with a slit on one side-dent in your jaw that looks like fingerprints: you fill that in with more blush until you have a higher cheek bone on one side. Also you have bags under your eyes. My all time favorite is the 101 Dalmatians look (one dark ring around one eye-with a little red in the middle).

So my thing is, put it out front-let a brotha know: 1) I don't want your money, 2) You don't ask me for my money, 3) You must have a job-I'm not funny or prejudiced-you can have a job driving a trash truck, it's a job, somebody's got to do it, 4) You don't ask me for my money, 5) Don't put your hands on me unless it is affectionate, 6) You don't ask me for my money, 7) If my children said you looked at them funny in a sexual manner or touched them, your ass got to go. Whether they are lying or not, I can always get another man, but I can't produce the same child again. They come first.

Is this too much to ask for? I mean you got to have rules and regulations. If not, you will lose everything and get your butt beat. So protect your assets: your children, your money and yourself.

# Chapter 3

My profession-I'm a correctional officer (I supervise female inmates-bad asses). But at 115 pounds-I get my respect. They called me Ms. Scott, because I don't let anything get by me. They wish I would go up for a promotion so I can supervise my fellow co-workers and leave them alone.

Oak Park State Prison has 400 to 450 employees. It is a maximum security prison. It holds up to 1200 inmates in the main unit and 200 inmates in the small unit on the back. We housed inmates that have committed the 7 deadly sins per our state law. We do get inmates that have committed lesser crimes but they are habitual violators and have been blessed with longer sentences. Yes we get the people who've committed murders, aggravated assault with and without a deadly weapon, involuntary and voluntary murder and sex offenders of all types. So we have a serious job.

In the institution, there is a program that they offer, the Residential Substance Abuse Program, it usually is mandated by the Department of Pardon and Parole before they can be released or let back into society. When I say let back into society, it may be projects, trailer parks, ghetto or the suburbs.

I began to observe that my inmates' behavior began to change. I mean you know us females, when something happens we change our appearances. Well they began to wear more make up and perfumed water. Usually they get hold of a magazine with a perfumed sample. They take it out and put it in water. They usually let the solution set a couple days. Then it becomes perfume. Anyway, it works for them. You would think we had cleaners that did alterations because their pants begin to fit tighter. Their uniforms were pressed and looked pure white. Even the nasty ones begin to take a shower in the morning.

Ms. Scott, they would say, they need to sell Massengill in the store, I may need it. I'm thinking, your ass been locked up for years without a douche, you need more than Massengill. You need a water hose and a 5 gallon bottle of vinegar. But I should have known it was a man that has caused this entire ruckus on my dorm.

Accountability, Security and Sanitation is my main focus as a dorm officer. We have to keep account of all inmates at all times. If one decides to go missing and we can't explain where she is, we could lose our jobs. Security-we have to make sure every door and gate is locked. We have to protect the public from them and them from the public. Yes, we have to protect them. Sanitation-it has to be clean. Inmates appear to act the way they live. If it is nasty they act nasty and vice versa. But there are some there is no help for.

One day an inmate decided she would invite me to their graduation. As the officer for the unit it was common that the officer attend the graduation that was assigned. So I said OK. The representative that felt the need to invite me was an inmate named Bailey. She was an elderly inmate. The judge does not have any sympathy on who he locks up these days. She was in her sixties. She was a pretty lady. She acted young for her age. She looked younger than the inmates in their forties. She would say, I just sold my merchandise-I did not use. Everyday Bailey with her prissy self was in my face, don't forget the graduation. She acted as if she was on a mission for the CIA. Finally she says don't you want to meet our counselor? I looked up and said excuse me with an attitude. She stated you heard what I said. She continued and said we all think you need a man in your life so you can lighten up. We got someone perfect that you can meet, she said. Then she tried to smooth it out and said you are young, pretty, nice figure and a great personality and I'm not trying to get in your business but you don't have a ring on your finger, word on the street says you don't have any children- thank god for that, she said under her breath. I said excuse me. She says you so serious all the time I know your children would think they were in boot camp, girl. So as she was finishing up I was thinking, do I look that desperate, can they tell I was going through the worst time in my life, oh my god one of these loose mouth officers have been spreading my business, because that's in the job description too.

Sometimes officers will be on the phone gossiping. Inmates sit at the table in the dayroom reading their lips. I believe some officers feel if they don't participate in Rumors, Gossips and Lies, they might not get a raise.

One of the things you can get fired for is personal dealings. Inmates should not help you get a man.

So, I stopped doing my paperwork and stood up-you see I am a straight up officer. What she just implied could get my job. Even though I was a little bit interested I had to check her ass which I was so famous for. I could curse an inmate out so quick she would forget why she got cursed out. All inmates knew that when I stand on the back of my legs, it is on. So I gave it to her. I stated in a nasty tone: I don't need anyone locked up to help me get anything, not to mention a man-and the only thing you need to do is your time and get your ass out and stay the hell out. That the reason you probably got your ass locked up in the first damn place was tending to someone else's damn business. When you get your ass out you can be Chuck Woolry and play Love Connection. So for now the only thing you need to do is do your time, get out and stay out and if you don't stop running that flap I'll put your ass under the lockdown. Bailey did a fake smile and stated honey, I'm just playing, please forgive me, I know I was out of line and please don't write me up. I didn't mean to make you hostile.

She sashayed off and went on about her business. When she approached the other inmates I overheard her say, and I knew she wanted me to hear it, you know you can't help black folks, especially them shit colored ones. She knows she needs a good dick; look at her she thinks her ass got it going on. I could not help but smile to myself. There's something about elderly inmates, you can't stay mad with them. But she needed to know to stay in her place. I don't care how old she is; the state made her an inmate.

I just did not need any Rumors, Gossip and Lies, especially among inmates.

# Chapter 4

At the graduation, I was sitting there going through the motions thinking, this is not me. How did I let them talk me into it? Well there was a part in the graduation when the inmates give out special awards. Guess what? They called my name. I went up and they gave me this beautiful certificate for giving them tough love. I mean I must say I gave their asses a lot of tough love. I baptized each and every one of them. They were crying to their counselors every day, especially that female counselor-I know I made her job hard. So naturally they wanted a speech. They put me on Front Street. At the end I stated the reason why I gave them tough love. It is for the children that you left at home. I continued by saying the following: you need to use what you have learned and what I put you through and remind yourself this is how prison is-it is tough. You need to stay home and take care of your babies. They need you. Drugs and Alcohol should never come between the loves you have for your children.

Inmates don't understand what children go through. I mean they are bullied and picked on. I have this little girl that I have taken up with. Her mother is in prison. Since the state decided to put inmates on the internet you can go online and pull up their picture. Well, would you know some smartass at school went on line? He pulled her mother's picture up, made copies, and passed them out. It devastated Shanique so, that the Principal called me at work and asked me to come and calm her down. She was trying to fight the whole class. Let me say this, it was an ugly picture of her momma too. So you know those kids had a field day. In the end of my speech, I received a standing ovation.

At the end of the program, a problem came up. We had to get an approval in order for me to keep the certificate. I was fine-knowing that I was recognized. It was no big deal.

Then there he was with the most gorgeous sexiest to die for smile-I mean a tall cool glass of lemonade in the middle of July. He looked like that cold water that Ms. Celia had in the Color Purple. The cold water before she spit in it. Remember when she spit in her husband's daddy's water before she gave to him? That was a nasty scene.

He was at least 6'5". He had a handsome light brown complexion. He wasn't too light. The sun did him justice. He had a cute mustache and goatee. A nice fade haircut, dark sexy brown eyes with a boyish grin to match that would just make you shake your head. You know how you wished Shemar Moore on the Young and the Restless had a million look-a-likes? Well here was one of them. He had on a black and white checkered suit that hung just right.

I said to myself, was I that occupied that I didn't see him during the graduation? How in the hell did I miss him? I was like Florida on Good Times "Damn, Damn and Damn". Where was he during the graduation program? Ohhhh. It hit me. He was the man that gave out the diplomas. He didn't look that good from where I was sitting. But I was sitting way in the back. Lord, Howard really got me voodoo, where I can't see other men. Am I that wrapped up in my job that I missed him through graduation?

I mean, I am observant. Then again, I was intentionally late for the program. Excuses, Excuses, and Excuses. But, that's not the issue right now, knowing who he is now.

He walked up to me and introduced himself. He said I am Michael Welch, the counselor of the graduating class. I said nice to meet you. We shook hands. I turned to walk away-that's when he offered to bring the certificate to my house. Being the officer I am who is always on the job, I looked him dead in the eyes and said that won't be necessary. If he only knew I could have raped his ass with everyone looking. Don't you know he was poisonous? Looking like a pretty ass cobra ready to strike. May I add I hadn't had any maintenance in three months-no tune up or oil change; tires had not been rotated or balanced. I'm sorry enough of that. I got on the short bus then. Damn, was he fine! It took an act of Congress not to smile. But somehow I managed to turn around and leave him standing there with everyone looking. I believe the Pacific Ocean took up in my panties and claimed residence, because I was wet between my legs.

Again, damn he was fine.

## Chapter 5

When I returned to work, the whole dorm was grinning from ear to ear-you know us females. When we accomplished a mission, we get a look of I told you so.

We should have been named No-males. The NO for nosey. It took me an hour to get them out of my business. They kept throwing out comments, statements, and questions. Department of Families and Children's Services must have taken up on my housing units. When you apply for benefits (food stamps and welfare), they want to know everything, even what color drawers you have on.

Then to make matters worse, what did Counselor Welch do? He brought his fine ass down the sidewalk to my dorm. The inmates knew he was coming. I should have picked up on the signals. They kept peeping out of their windows and whispering. Just like the projects. You can ride by above the speed limit at any time of the night or day, some one is always looking. They can give you a detailed description of your vehicle, how many in the car, what they had on, and what they were doing. But when the police asked them-they didn't see anything.

It was lockdown time. This is when all inmates return to their cells and get locked in. We do an official count to make sure all inmates are present and have not escaped. My one last wish before I retire is for an inmate to escape and I am driving the perimeter car.

See, the perimeter car monitors the area outside of the prison. An officer drives it around the prison-24 hours and 7 days a week. It is there to prevent escapes. When she climbs over the fence, I will be waiting. So, I can put that .38 Caliber all in her ass. That's a freebie. You officially get paid to shoot someone, legally.

At this time, we as officers get a chance to eat and catch up on paperwork, or just take a breather. Mr. Welch felt the need to want to make rounds. This man has been a counselor for this unit for two months.

I have never seen him before. Now, he is interested in his dorm. Now picture this, ninety two inmates, one hundred and eighty-four eyes and ears all in your business. They were looking out of their cell windows. I mean, these heifers can read lips through steel. Six Million Dollar Man ain't got anything on them. I'm wondering if this brother looks this good all the time. Hell what does the family tree look like? I know it took the Son, Father and the Holy Ghost to keep me from melting away. I had some hellified willpower to stay focused. So, I maintained my professionalism.

I stopped him in his tracks. I said, look, I'm not looking for a boyfriend. I just had a breakup. I don't need anyone coming around my children. I can tell he wasn't studying anything I just said. That probably made him happier. He probably was just looking for a booty call. Now this brother was good. He said in a business tone, I just came to check on the dorm. I know they've been complaining about security. I told him well you need to get with my supervisor. He said I'm getting with you. He continued by saying I just want you to know that you are doing a good job. Finally he said if any problems occur, please call me. I'll be checking on you and the dorm from time to time. But don't let me stop you from eating your lunch. He said I'll be in touch.

In Waiting to Exhale there was a scene written by Terry McMillan when she was walking away back to her house and she said I hope he's not watching me walk away and she looked back and he was looking. I wanted to watch him walk away. Since DFACS was in the window looking I had to play it off and look quickly.

# Chapter 6

I told you this brother was good. He conveniently called me every day off and on. He even visited the dorm. He had questions about the inmates and their behavior. Or asked would I make announcements from time to time to the dorm regarding the program. If he didn't call, I could just tell I was getting addicted. I conveniently got on the inmates' behinds and threatened to call him especially when they slipped. They would say oh he ain't here today or he is up there in his office. Oh, but you already know that don't you Ms. Scott. I gave one inmate two hours of extra duty. We can give an inmate work instead of writing a disciplinary report for small infractions. If I need my dorm clean I can work her like a Hebrew slave.

My fellow officers would often inquire about him. They would say girl is he married? The following are their favorite comments: 1) he can come on my dorm and sit in my lap with his good looking self, and 2) If he looks that good with his clothes on what does he look like with them off? I knew all of this was to see would I get jealous. No, I didn't bite into it at all. I grew up with nosey people, who were professionals at being in my business.

I guess he got tired of me dodging him and running from him whenever he got too friendly. He entered my dorm. I could smell the Kenneth Cole cologne he was wearing. He approached me and he went in for the kill. He said look can I get your phone number. I politely said no. He said why. I looked him up and down with an evil look and said I do not date my coworkers. He said I'm not a coworker; I'm a counselor-a contract counselor and you work for the state. I said we both are employed by Oak Park State Prison. So that means we are coworkers. He looked at me and said it's been two months, I have shown great patience and one thing I have is patience. He then said you are gonna give in, one day and I am going to be waiting.

I said there are approximately 150 women that work here, why don't you pick one of them. He said I did, I picked you. Inmate Bailey's sneaky ass was standing by the wall eavesdropping and smiling worse than the Grinch who stole Christmas. Welch got up, walked to the door, smiled, and said I'll see you when you get off.

Bailey said he told you didn't he and walked off grinning. I knew her-she was going to report in like Rona Barrett of the Projects to the rest of the inmates. I didn't waste any time by getting her straight after making that comment. I had him to worry about. I didn't want to see him later or at all.

At the end of my shift, I began to sweat. Oh my god I know he ain't gonna be standing by my car when I get off work. I know he's not gonna try to catch me on the way up to sign out. I was thinking hard. I got to find a way so he won't see me. So I said, I know, I'll go through the gym. He wouldn't see me through his classroom window. Then I'll go through administration so he won't catch me in the lobby. I had a master plan. Yeah, that's it. I'll do that. Thinking why am I scared? I am the great Ms. Scott, nobody scares me. What am I running for, who does he think he is. Shit, I'll curse his ass out if he is out by my car. I mean I'll happily curse his ass out.

Meanwhile the RSAP or the Residential Substance Abuse Program class was returning back to the dorm. I asked them what ya'll back for. We got out early today. I didn't think much about it. Then I noticed that my dorm was getting quiet-real quiet. Someone pulled at my door. I was assuming it was my relief. It was 2:00 pm. It was the end of my shift. I popped the door and kept writing. I smelled that cologne; again-it was him. I said to myself, what the hell? I was stunned. My mouth was wide open. I heard an inmate say you can close your mouth now Ms. Scott. He stood there smiling and said I decided to walk you out just in case you tried to disappear. I said to myself I'll be goddamn. This m********f****** is too damn good. I had my escape route all planned out. He f****** my shit up.

So my relief came. Michael waited patiently, pretending to interact with the inmates. Just as I was getting ready to exit, I thought he was in one of those deep conversations with a resident where he could not put her off. He excused himself from the conversation. though, and followed me out the door. I glanced over my shoulder and looked back at the dorm. In the window was nothing but big smiles and eyes. They were high fiving and pointing. If I had a brick and could get away it, I would've thrown it at them. But I knew I didn't have any money to give the state for a window.

As we walked up the sidewalk, he asked why are you so stubborn and mean. He said you got this wall up, nobody's gonna hurt you. He said you are so attractive and strong I just want to get to know you. Can I get to know you? Can we be friends? I was taking it all in, because as you see he was trying to stay in control of the conversation with all those questions. I said I don't have a problem getting to know you. I just don't want any drama in my life, especially on the job drama-that is the worst kind, I said. I just don't socialize with the people I work with, especially when I go home. I don't need to see them. What most of my coworkers do is get in your business. They want to visit you, see how you live, whether you're broke or not, what kind of man you're dating, or are your children bad. Next thing you know you're on the prison news channel. For me it's a good practice I said. I don't gossip and I don't want them gossiping about me. Since you have been coming to my dorm-the whole institution has been on alert. They all went to Code Red. People called me that never call. They're so fake, it is pitiful. They don't know how to be tactful. They are just as ghetto as hell. But anyway, that's my story, why I don't participate in socialization with coworkers. I caught him off guard, because he couldn't respond. He was quiet as we walked.

I went in the office to sign out; I thought he would go on about his business. But he stood outside waiting. I was really getting pissed, because now my coworkers were taking notice. My supervisors were looking at me in a strange way. I could tell they were whispering about us. I have bold coworkers. They don't care if you hear them talk. They want you to hear. So I walked real fast as if I had fire in my drawers. He was trying to keep up with those Payless Shoe Store shoes on. He did good, too. When we got outside in the parking lot, he said you are serious; you don't want anyone to know that I like you. I said yes. He said let me call you at home. I said didn't you just hear me? I said I don't want to socialize with the people I work with. Seeing that everyone was coming out to the parking lot, I really was on pins and needles. I said look let's talk about this later, I really got to go. He said to me BYE Peaches. I said what did you call me? Peaches, that's my name for you.

He said I will be calling you tonight. I was nosey then-you don't have my number. He said yes I do. I asked how did you get it. Don't worry about that I got it. I asked what is it. When he quoted my number, I was furious. The only thing I could say was you better not call my damn house, I'll curse you out. He said we'll see, I've been cursed out before. I drove off. My Honda couldn't go fast enough.

All the way home I couldn't help but think of how did he get my number? Whoever gave him my number gonna be in deep shit. Ooh, that's scandalous. I don't know him like that, he might have cleared the background check for the state, but he still may be a pervert. I've got girls to think about. He is ambitious and determined though, in a sick kind of way. I mean I wasn't friendly, nice, polite, or courteous toward his yellow ass. He keeps coming back like the Energizer Bunny. Something is wrong with him I can't put my finger on it. I wanna know who let light skinned brothers make a comeback anyway.

## Chapter 7

When I arrive home, I always take off my uniform, take a shower and wait for the phone to ring. My children participate in sports all year. So I lived at the school house. But I did check the caller ID to see did Mr. Welch call. Every time the phone rang, my heart skipped a beat. So when my children called and said they were ready to be picked up, I flew down the road to pick them up. One of my daughter's friends needed a ride home. Being that I'm like a team mom, I took her home. Because I would not dare leave a child outside waiting on a ride, it is too dangerous. Especially if I could do something about it, I would want someone to do the same for me. Sometimes, I even would wait there until their ride comes. I was a caring mother. But today was different; a man might call my house. I needed to be home, just in case. I needed to really bounce back from the breakup.

Then the light came on in my mind-I thought you weren't interested? You don't need a man in your life right now. You said you need to get to know yourself. You need to get closer to the Lord, before you start dating. Here you are lusting over a man. You can't even wait for him to call. You are supposed to be hard. What would your ex say (he would say you couldn't wait to give that ass up). The children would say mommy I thought you were gonna wait awhile before you start dating. My mother would say you need a man so your ass can lighten up and help pay your bills. I was having all kinds of thoughts. What would my coworkers think? What would he say? I can see him now. He would be saying shit like I know I could get into them drawers, she is not as tough as she puts on, your mouth said one thing-but your body said another. With everything I was thinking it hit me-hell he ain't even called my ignorant ass yet. I needed to get a grip. See, I do a lot of thinking when I'm driving. So I dismissed any thoughts out of my mind. I went back to business as usual.

As my day went on helping with homework, cooking supper, cleaning, and preparing for the next day at work, I got my usual phone calls from my friends or associates. They wanted to know the progress I've been making. In other words, they were just being nosey. So I became private not telling them everything. I didn't want them to know in a few months I would be leaving my dream home. My kids and I will be officially foreclosed on. The realtors were so nice. They gave us a few months to live there until tax season. So we could find another home. Howard would not take his name off of the mortgage so I could refinance the house in my name.

I was getting ready to make sure the children took a real bath. I've got one child that would go in there and run the water like he was bathing, he must think I'm stupid. The second one would go in there and sit in the water. The third one goes in and three minutes she's out. So I have to do bath detail. Before you let the water out I need to see it. I need to see if the water is dirty and the tub has a ring. If that didn't satisfy me I need to smell them to see if they smell like Dove soap.

The phone rang-it was Lessie, my biological mother. I usually don't pick up. But she called back. I lied; I said I didn't hear the phone I was in the bathroom. She said anyway some man called here named Mr. Welch he said he'll call you back. I said who. She said you heard me, when did you start living in a tree-you ain't no owl. In a hostile tone she said you need to give your own phone number out; I am not your secretary and she hung up. It seems I stopped breathing. I called her back and said did he leave a number? She said there's one on the caller ID, you want it? I said yes. She gave it to me. She said I know it's not a bill collector because you never asked for the numbers before.

When we hung up, I thought if he called me back I won't be there. I wandered how did he get that number? Shit I don't want Lessie with her big mouth ass asking him questions. So I made up an excuse to visit her. I knew I had mail there so I called her back and asked did I have any. She said yes, I know you didn't call me for that. I told her I would be over in a few minutes and hung up. All I have to do is bring up some gossip and that would buy me enough time so Welch can call me back, because she loves to gossip.

When I entered she gave me my mail; I asked how everybody was doing. She looked up through the cloud of smoke she just blew out. Lessie had been smoking as long as I been in the world. There's one thing I know; do not come between her and a pack of Kool Miles 100 in the box-the short cigarettes. I asked her about the child in my daughter's class that had gotten pregnant. She lit up. Her second favorite thing is gossiping. She gave me past, present and the future. She knew everything, even down to explicit details. In the end, she always says you have to put children in the hands of the Lord. Especially disobedient children who think they are grown, they need to be on their own. That's what I did for y'all. Y'all started having babies; I put y'all's asses out and gave you to the Lord. I know he didn't want you but I didn't either. I ignored what she said because I knew she was lying about not wanting us. I looked up at the clock. It was 9:50 pm, past my children's bedtime which was 9:00. He hadn't called yet. So I asked her to let me get his number so I can return his call. She told me to check the caller ID. She remembered and said, I gave you that damn number already, damn you got it bad.

Let us talk about the caller ID. I don't know who invented the caller ID. They need to get a Purple Heart or a Nobel Peace Prize. The caller ID is serious. Just when you thought *69 was a stroke of genius. I mean it is so serious that even my 78 year old grandmother who doesn't know a lot about technology except to turn things off and on, figured the caller ID out. Shoot, when the phone rings, she would get up during the stories or soap operas and walk to the back of her trailer to my cousin's room which has a caller ID and check to see who is calling. She will not pick up the phone before she checks it. Of course, usually by the time she would get to it the ringing has stopped. Now that is serious.

While I'm at it, let me tell you bill collectors something. When you call anybody and they don't pick up on the third ring, you might as well go on to the next person to call. You need to please hang up. The caller ID is on the job. We know it's you, especially when we see private name or unavailable showing up on the screen. That's why they invented anonymous caller rejection block, so you have to say who you are. So just put your name on the screen. We do not have any money.

We do not need to be reminded that we owe you. If we had money you would not have to call. We would have paid you already. So do you think that by calling us that will make us as the consumer come in and pay you quicker? Hell no. Can I get an AMEN somebody?

When I checked, his whole name was there. I thought, he didn't block his number. He called from home. That's a good sign. He can't be married. What man would call from his home? He must live at home with his momma (a scrub). So I wasn't ready to let him know my real number. So I sneaked and called from Lessie's house. I tried to block the number but Bellsouth wouldn't let me. So I called direct. See, it's polite to return someone's phone calls. That's how I was raised. Who am I fooling? I knew deep down inside, I just wanted to call him.

A woman answered. I asked could I speak to Mr. Welch. She said OK. He answered. I asked him, you called me? He said yeah I told you I was gonna call when I got home. I could hear her in the background interrogating him. Finally he told me to hold on. I could hear him tell her this is my coworker. I was checking in with her. She didn't buy it. Because when he returned to me he said I'll talk to you when I get to work. I said OK THEN.

There is an old country story about a bird. There was a bird in a cage hanging on the porch. A strong wind came by and blew the cage off of the hook. When the cage hit the ground, it just fell apart. The bird stood up, walked around, and looked at the cage. The bird just shook his head and said "Cheap, Cheap, Cheap," That was me "Cheap, Cheap and Cheap".

When I hung up I was completely confused. Automatically I thought the worse; I know his m********* ass is not married. He's got some nerve. A woman must be living with him. I know one thing-when I see his highlighter ass tomorrow he's gonna get the sermon of his life. With that I gathered up my children and drove home.

When I arrived home, I asked myself, if I was totally against getting to know him why did I call him?

# Chapter 8

Next day, I went to the dorm as usual knowing he would come in to work at 8:00 am. So, I had time to prepare. I definitely was ready. I was gonna be like Johnnie Cochran the attorney on his ass.

Wouldn't you know it? He called me at 6:00 am. The Control room operator called and told me to stand by for an outside phone call. All our calls have to be prescreened through the supervisor. So it had to be important for some one to call me at work. I thought maybe one of my children was sick. As I hesitated to answer, I calmed down. It was him. I asked where are you. He said I'm at home. I'm sorry for her being ignorant last night. He said, she's just crazy like that. I told him I would be too if a woman called my house. He said that's my house and she knows what time it is.

I told you something was wrong with him. I knew it. I knew it. I know you been waiting on this part-I know if you were a jury you would have tried and sentenced him. I know some of you would have given him the death penalty. I am going to be real. I am not going to sugarcoat it. He's married. You probably already knew that. See, I ride the short bus from time to time. But I never have driven it. I know you know what the short bus is. I'll explain. The short bus is for special people who have minor mental difficulties. They can function on their own. But ten percent of the time they don't see the whole picture-someone has to help them, and when you find out it is too late.

He clearly states, we are roommates. Because of the children we stay together. I stopped him and said look I don't talk to married men. The Lord would not be pleased. I hung up the phone. I knew he would call again. Pretty boys don't like to be rejected.

It seemed as if whenever he called or stopped by, Inmate Bailey was somewhere close by, grinning. I continued on my day. He showed up on my dorm at 7:55 am. He looked as if he was desperate. He gave me a white bag and a cup of coffee. I brought you breakfast. He said we need to talk. If you had let me talk to you yesterday, I would have explained to you what is going on. Then whatever you decide I'll go with it. I just know I want to see you. He walked out of the dorm. Just like I said, pretty boys don't like to be rejected.

Now in the beginning all my inmates were happy that he was talking to me. Now them bitches trying to act jealous-I can't win for losing. Finally, I had to lock one of their asses up for being insubordinate. She knew to never disrespect an officer verbally. They always are trying to find some way to get over. It's a shame you got to check grown ass people. They forget they are inmates. I didn't put them in jail and I'm not gonna let them out. But while they are here, they belong to me. They need to follow the rules and regulations and give me respect. They can cut out all that sarcasm and throwing out innuendos. I meant just that.

He called me at noon and asked can we meet? I explained to him I'm not interested in knowing your dirty laundry. He said well I'll call you when I get home. I asked him how did you get my number. He explained that the tool control officer owed him a favor and he went in the control room and gave him the number. I was furious. When I see Kevin I'm gonna kick his ass. He knows that's against policy. He should at least ask my permission. He begged me not to say anything. I lied. I won't say anything, not one word. He just didn't know I was going to say curse words that the Webster Dictionary will not ever print.

Lessie called me again and gave me his message that he called. I told her I'll call him back. Knowing good damn well I was not going to call him back. I should have known Lessie would not hold out. See, I was on my regular days off. She broke down on Saturday morning and told him that I didn't live there and asked did he want my number? When my telephone rung at 9:00 am, I thought it was my ex. He tries to catch me when I am half way asleep so he can get something over on me. But it was Welch. I said Damn don't you get the message. He said no I don't. He also said I told you I was patient. He asked how are you doing? I looked at the phone and told him this was not a good time, I had company. He asked when are they leaving? I said none of your business. He said girl stop lying if you had company you would not have answered the phone. I said OK and hung up. He called back and I didn't pick up. Instead I turned my ringer off and went back to sleep. He left several messages asking me out to lunch. So we could talk away from the job.

But the devil was busy. He constantly whispered in my ear. What can it hurt? Loneliness is a sad affair. You are alone. You know you need a good dick. Besides if he is married that means you don't have to be bothered. You said you don't want a relationship. This would be for convenience. Girl, be a player. Remember how you just got played. A man in a wheelchair played your ass. See, Welch can't stay long, because he has to go home. That means you can leave your options open to see other people. Just let him know you do not want a commitment. You just want to be friends. One thing, definitely you don't want anybody to know. If anybody found out, that little angel image that your family have of you will go down the toilet.

See, I gave up being an usher in the church I was raised up in because I was living with Howard. That's why I was pressuring him to get married. We were not living right in God's eyes. Here it goes again; I'm going against my faith because I'm hurting.

I played hard to get over the weekend. I would not answer his phone calls or return any. I said to myself if he still wants to talk to me then he will beg. I knew if I didn't talk to him-he would. I do have my pride. I don't need to give up so quickly.

## Chapter 9

After I had run out of stall maneuvers and after playing hide and go seek, he called me and asked me out for lunch. I agreed. It was my day off, so I decided to meet him in mutual territory. So we met in the prison parking lot. It was the fall time of the year and it had begun to get cool. He was totally shocked. See, my uniform does not do me justice. I don't like bragging. So what if he doesn't know I'm just as cocky and arrogant as he is. But I have a voluptuous set of d-cup titties and a nice round ass to match. I had on the perfect outfit. I had on an off-white thick turtle neck sweater with a pair of Levi Jeans. May I add, they both were tight on my body. He was speechless. Finally I told him you don't have to say anything; I can see it on your face. He has on his usual shirt with a tie and slacks. We rode in his SUV (A black 2002 Lincoln Navigator). The conversation was good. Finally he asked why you look so different at work than now. He said you don't look like the woman I work with. I replied that's the answer, I'm not at work. I am there to do a job. I keep work and pleasure separated. When I walked through the gate I am about business. It's a game. I planned to win so I can go home to my family. So, when I do leave I smile to myself. I know I have won, because I am going home to my family at the end of the day. I rest peacefully at night. Then the next day I start all over again.

Since the restaurants are very limited we agreed to eat Chinese in a nearby town. It was lunchtime. We ate the buffet. Before we began to eat he asked me to say the blessing. It was a shame because I never say blessing. My son always says it. I forgot the words. I make my children say it but I don't do it. I played it off and asked since it was your idea for lunch you do it. If there is a next time I'll do it. Luckily he agreed. As he finished he added Lord I just want to thank you for allowing Ms. Scott to have lunch with me. I smiled.

After, that he called me every day two or three times. When I worked he walked me out to my car. He called me in the morning to make sure I was getting ready for work. He was so concerned. He admired me for being a hard working single mother. I often expressed to him how much my children came first. He often asked about the children's activities. He would ask could he go to the games with me. But I wasn't ready for that. I mean I had my doubts. Believe me I was raised in a Methodist church and I have already been scorned by having three of my children out of wedlock. I tossed and turned thinking nobody would have expected this kind of behavior out of me. My family, friends, or kids wouldn't have. I am dating married men, now. But I was tired of putting everything in a relationship and coming up short. My kids and I suffer.

Past relationships were with single men that claimed they wanted to take care of me and my kids. But they worked so hard to get me and as soon as they got me, I become a trophy on the mantle piece or a special edition Barbie. When you buy it, you take it out, look at it, and put it back in the box. All I ever required was quality time. My break-ups weren't because they were cheating on me. It was administrative issues. Why do I have to be a wife, when you are trying not to marry me? If you want to tell me who can ride in my car or visit me at home, pay the bills.

I have lots of friends that have all tested this water, dating married men. Some were successful and some failed horribly. But they all agreed, don't let your feelings get caught up and you got it made. Married men can be a gold mine-that is, if you find the right one who is a paymaster.

All those years, I have been totally against it. I would say to my friends, if and when two people stand up before the reverend, congregation, and God and commit to say those vows, no one should violate that. No matter what. That ceremony is a sacred thing. That's why Howard showed me separation papers before we started dating.

I wasn't looking for anything permanent to bring home to the family. My family gets attached too easy. Lessie is still good friends with two of my children's crack head daddy. We have been separated for 13 years. My family has been trying to marry me off for years. They say I am too damn independent. One of my friends told me if I could afford it

I would probably hire an escort from to time to take care any sex if I needed it.

To sum it up, my children succeeding is my priority. Nothing comes before them. I have never shacked up or slept with men when they are home. Due to Howard being paralyzed I believe they assumed we were just sleeping together and that he couldn't function at all. He was the first and only that I ever had lived with. Ooh, but if walls could talk. They accepted the situation. But I always reminded them this is a temporary situation. It is wrong for a man and woman to live together. When Howard and I built our home we met with the children and explained we would be marrying in a year. As you can see, that never happened.

This is how serious that I loved my kids. I don't have problems with a man disciplining my children. But if one of them told me that they have been molested in any way, size, shape, and form, that nigger got to go. The children come first. I can always get another boyfriend but I can't get another child named Josh, Cameron, Sean, and Kira. When my children become grown and out of my house the rules change. They are grown. They are out on their own. I might let him explain his side of the story why he was touching my child after I shoot him. But other than that, he will be a statistic of murder and/or aggravated assault with a deadly weapon.

See, all my children make good grades and are star athletes in their respective sports. They compete in all kinds of sports all year long. Whether it is at school or for recreation, they have a lot of extracurricular activities. Scholarships are in the making so you have to stay focused. You can't lose them, unless the Lord takes them. Even, if it means giving up your personal life to do it. When I conceived them, I didn't hear a little voice saying I'm ready to come in the world. Only thing I heard was this is the best stuff I ever had. Until, I got pregnant.

So, children didn't ask to come in the world. So, why do we have to mistreat them or deprive them because we want to live our lives? Especially so we can have a man. It's not fair. I attend all their functions, no matter where it is. I traveled all over the state just to see my kids perform. I'm usually the only black parent in the bleachers. Letting some of the white parents know yes, I am representing all black kids on the team and the white ones too that are not prejudiced when their parents are not there. I knew they couldn't stand my ass. But ask me did I care. Hell no. If I had to do it again, I sure would.

In the meantime, I barely get child support. All one father had to pay was $185.00. He wouldn't keep a job. He would have the nerve to say if they need anything you can ask my momma and daddy. Hell I didn't fuck his momma and daddy. What would I look like, asking them? They didn't ask for my p*****, you did.

Since, I'm one of those single parents that want to be different, once I end a relationship it's over. No booty calls, phone calls, or good conversation. Since I wasn't giving up the ass, my absent parent felt he didn't have to pay child support. He would not work. When child support was getting ready to do a review this rascal would get a low paying job so they can figure up his child support. He would say I'm not giving you any money so another man can live off of you. I had them to let him know the money goes toward your children. If you want p*****, that's extra. Ain't nothing free.

With that we went on our separate ways. I wasn't going to give in. We will do without. The Lord will make a way. In the meantime he is doing worse than me. So women don't give him any. The bible states the Lord will take care of the little children. You as an adult, on the other hand, are another story, if the Lord takes care of you.

## Chapter 10

After several phone calls and lunches, I was really feeling him. But I asked myself where does a man really fit in my life? How can I give him quality time? Sure, some men start out acting like they are interested in the children's activities. But somewhere it gets old. Howard was different. Due to being in a wheelchair, he didn't want to go out. He just knew I was with the kids and as long as I crawled in his bed he was alright.

I've read that married men prey on women like me because they know we are too busy to ask more of their time and commitment. I can see that, too. Time and commitment we don't have much of, if you have kids. Men today want you to choose. They would say I'm first. Family, friends, activities, church and yes children come second. The only thing they will negotiate with is your job. That's because they are not trying to give you too much of their money.

Somewhere in all my thinking, I agreed to make a deal with the devil. It really didn't take much to make this deal. I can see Bishop T.D. Jakes staring down at me and saying you need to run to Jesus and stop running to man. He is the only man you need. But all I wanted was a little companionship, not much. I won't disrespect her marriage that much. I even will have him home at a decent hour. I will not call her house. He doesn't need to spend the night because of my kids. Shoot, I will even encourage him to work out their problems. We will be friends with an additional benefit, sex. I just needed this comfort for a short while. I know how to go to the altar and repent when I finish.

When he called me, I acted as if I was upset, because I didn't want him to really know that I wanted to see him. I told him that I was really getting to know him and was enjoying his company. I just didn't know if I could keep seeing him. I think we really needed to cool off.

The truth be told, I have been faithful to a man with a disability only to be rejected. Only to be told he is not ready to get married. I thought who in the fuck does he think he is? If you can't get a man in a wheelchair to marry you, you must be pitiful. Because if I could get a hold of that wheelchair I know I'd cut them tires. Or maybe I'd just take those screws out and when he is rolling in his wheelchair, it would just collapse. (SMILE)

One thing about life: when someone tells you that you can't have something it will make you want it more. You won't stop until you get it. No matter how bad it may be for you. When you reject someone it will either do one of two things: 1) They'll leave you alone and talk about you, or 2) They will see can they get you –they need to know what makes you so special that you are not giving in.

As, I knew he would do, I reported to work and he called. I listened how he clearly gives his $20.00 player explanation. He just didn't know I paid my membership dues to the player's club too. So I listened attentively. Just after he finished making the statement that he was, indeed married, he said things weren't working out between them. He said they were just roommates. He talked about how she criticized him in his role as a father and a husband. I said how do you and her continue to live together with all that anger. I told him I was sorry to hear that. I calmly stated but you and her need to think about the kids and work out your differences. He replied I know how to be a father without living in the house with my children. I knew then that Welch was not planning on leaving his wife. I wanted to see how he really felt about her, because he gave the standard answers. He knew he would have the best of both worlds.

Later on Welch came into work. He made rounds on the living unit. I broke the news to him. I don't know where this is going but I will agree to see you but there are a few things need to be understood: 1) I don't need you getting attached to my kids, 2) I don't want your money & don't ask me for mine, 3) If I have time to see you I will, don't ask me to make changes in my schedule, 4) I am very popular in this area- the town I lived in is surrounded by four counties. I am well known in each and everyone of them. Georgia has 180 counties. That leaves you 175 to play in, 5) Don't be tracking me down like you are the FBI, and 6)If you need to spend the night with me-you need to pay for an hotel. I thought I did well. We agreed and shook hands. He just didn't know; I knew I would be temporary forever. I just don't need to get caught up.

After we agreed I had to test him. It is something I do that tells me if he's really interested. Everyone is impressed with the standard things (cards, flowers and gifts). It is expected. So I wanted that too. But I was different. So I asked Counselor Welch would he bring me a couple of things on his way to work. I would have put my pay check on it that he would have forgotten or just was not going to do it. I said bring me a Tropicana Orange Juice (not from concentrate) and a Krispy Kreme Chocolate Donut. I told him they are sold at the BP station. He said, is that all? I will do anything for you he said. He knew exactly what I was talking about. See ladies men always forget the small things. I know you can relate. If he remembers he has potential.

Guess what, I was working some inmates on sidewalk detail-It was 8:30 am and he had not shown up yet. Now you know how my mind was going, he knew he wasn't coming to work anyway-at 8:40 am I saw him. I didn't see any green and white bag or even a small brown bag, as he was going to his office. At 8:45 am, he comes out of his office wearing my favorite colors. He had that walk as if he was walking on clouds. He was wearing a long sleeved deep purple colored shirt and a taupe print colored silk tie. Taupe colored pants to match. As he was walking towards me, I couldn't help but feel warm all over. He had that lemonade smile again. When he stepped into my space, he said I was late because I stopped at three stores-nobody had your kind of donuts ready. I called to let you know-you can check with the control room operator-she can tell you I called. I'm thinking yeah right; your ass probably didn't look at a store. Nice try. He continued on by saying but when I get off work I'll go to the Krispy Kreme and get you a whole box. But here is the orange juice and would I take this as a substitute. He said this is to let you know I was thinking about you. In his hand was a bag of Hershey chocolate kisses.

Now this brother was good. He had to be the vice-president or the treasurer of the Player's Association. He definitely was a professional. So I knew I had to step up my game. If I had been white, you could have named me little red riding hood. I was red all over. He just walked off and left me with a goofy look on my face. If he had a theme song, it would be the song Set It Off and he would be doing the bus stop all the way back to his office.

## Chapter 11

The next few months, I was like Dorothy in the Wizard of OZ. I didn't want to wake up. We had become best friends. The best part was he didn't pressure me into having sex. I had a secret. He was married. I did everything to try to keep the relationship anonymous. But the more I tried to keep him a secret, the more he kept trying to come out of the closet. I would plan for us to meet in private places for lunch and dinner.

One day I had to go pay my hairdresser. Moria owned Moria's House of Styles. She had a good business which has allowed her to afford two kinds of BMWs. He rode with me. I looked at him like a mother to her child and said do not get out. He says I'm not getting out. I go in and was talking to my hairdresser. I heard something at the door. I looked up. It was him standing there smiling. So I had to introduce him to the whole beauty salon. Now, I know the next time I go back to get my hair done, I will be interrogated.

When we were back in the car and ready to leave, I pretended I had left something inside so I could go back in. Each and every one in there thought he was so handsome and had a nice personality. I was happy, but I still had something to hide.

At Christmas, we had a romantic dinner and exchanged gifts. We ate at an Italian restaurant in downtown Williamsville. He ordered a Chardonnay (a white wine). I was shocked at my gifts. He gave me a sterling silver anklet with dolphins on it. If that wasn't enough he gave me a certificate for Toys-R-US for the kids. I gave him a Kenneth Cole's watch since he loved the cologne. We had great conversation. But I was sad and disappointed. Because after he left me, I knew I would be alone and he would be with her. It was something about starting the night out with someone- you want to wake up with that person. Or you want to know if he would be in someone else's arms.

No middle aged woman wants to be alone on Valentine's Day, Christmas Eve, Christmas Night, and New Years Eve. As a matter of fact no woman wants to be alone at these times. Depression had begun to set in my mood.

I wondered how he was celebrating Christmas Eve with her. Were they sitting by the Christmas tree cuddling up? Or were they exchanging gifts after they made love. Was he thinking of me at all? Are they being the happy couple, the couple he said that doesn't live in their house anymore? Are Shondrae, Cameron, and Christopher (his kids) enjoying their family moments? I know it must be nice. Having both parents at home showing how much they love them. The one thing that I couldn't give my children was a family with two parents.

I shouldn't feel guilty, but my children are young. They wouldn't understand that I had to give up the life with their fathers. I would have been a crack head if I stayed with the first one and the other one wouldn't know commitment if it shot him. I wouldn't have them back if they were the last two men on earth. I know they feel the same way about me too. I just want my money in the mailbox. Don't get me wrong-if they want to spend time with my kids, I am ok with that. All I ask is don't ask to spend time with me.

Depression had set in, but somehow he must have known I was feeling lonely. Because at 12:00 am, the phone rang, it was him; I could hear the kids in the background laughing. He said Merry Christmas and I love you. I said Merry Christmas and I love you too. He said I wish I could be there. I heard the kids say Daddy who is that. He said maybe your stepma. I said why did you say that? He said it's true, you know you like the sound of it. I said Yeah. I said where is your wife? He said in the other room. I said you know you're wrong. He said I know. I thought I know if the Lord is keeping a diary on me, this one will definitely be written down-talking to him while she was home. He said but what can I do, I want to be with you. He said I just wanted to say I was thinking about you and I can't wait to see you. He hung up. Depression packed up and went away. I was again on cloud nine. Sleep took me away.

The kids woke up early opening up toys and so did he. I mean he called me at 5:30 am. He was sounding like Santa Claus. He said what are you doing today. I said spending time with the family and kids. He said good. He said as long as you are not with another man. I said you are with her. He said she's just here. I said anyway. He said I'll be calling you back off and on, so stay near the phone.

He called me again later in the day. We talked off and on all day. We discussed what the children got for Christmas and how happy they were. If he got a phone call, he would not hang up. All he was doing was blocking. He knows he can't be here with me-so he's doing the next best thing. During one of our phone calls, we watched an entire football game together. We commented on every play like two old buddies. Shoot, she even got in on the conversation as she walked into the room. She apparently heard him make a comment about a play because she said tell who you are talking to that you're just mad because you can't play football anymore. Then he was trying to repeat what she told him. I said I heard her. That is how we spent Christmas and New Years on the telephone.

# Chapter 12

Each and every time, I always made sure that we were not alone. I wasn't ready for the sex. I was just trying to feel him out. We had agreed to go to Cameron's game together. I told him to meet me at the house at 6:00 pm. He shows up at 4:30 pm just as I was getting ready for my shower. I turned the TV on and asked him to stay in the living room. I told him don't be rambling around while I'm gone. He smiled. I'm not going to do anything out here, I promise.

When I came out of the shower, he was standing in my bedroom. I said I told you to stay in the living room. He said I know I heard something-I said stop lying with a smile. I walked by him to go to my dresser to get some panties. He came up behind me. I didn't know what to do. I had dreamed and hoped for this moment. But I hoped he would have moved out from her before we crossed this line.

He grabbed me from behind. Even though my robe was thick, it seems as if it wasn't there. His hands were slowly rubbing over my breasts. My nipples hardened up-begging to be touched. He kissed the back of my neck and my earlobes. My knees began to feel weak. He turned me around and gently kissed me on the lips. He had the softest lips. My robe came loose and fell open. He stepped back and admired my body. He unzipped his pants. I reached in his briefs and pulled him out. He picked me up as if to carry me to the bed. My legs were wrapped around him. I could hardly breathe. But I felt his hardness attempting to pry inside me. My pussy was so tight. It felt as if he tore inside. I caught my breath trying not to scream. It was the best pain I've felt in years. I have never made love in this position, standing up. It felt so good.

As I begin to climax, he said don't cum yet, I'm not ready for you to. He began to walk to the bed. He was still inside of me. He said I'll tell you when to cum. He laid me on the bed. As he lay on top of me, my legs still wrapped around his waist, he began to stroke my vagina.

He would go slow and then fast. I held on to him enjoying the ride. I did not feel any more pain. It seemed the moment would last forever. Then he whispered now you can cum. I kept cumin until my body trembled all over.

That's when I felt him gripping my cheeks tighter and he released his juices. I could feel his juices hit the back of my vagina. We were sweaty and breathing hard. We laid there as one. Our hearts beat together like Boyz to Men singing a cappella. He said this is not a booty call, this was love making. He knew I wasn't ready to come back to reality.

Even though this was a memorable moment it was a bitter sweet moment that we shared. It was the last good time I will have in this house. All the bad memories from what happened between Howard and I seemed to disappear. I gave the Realtors notice that we would be moving by the end of the month. My grandmother had agreed for us to live with her until we found another house. Yes, another house. I was raised in a house and that's what I want my kids to live in. I know it would be cramped living with grandma but we'll make it through. I had met this agent who works with people with bad credit. She was very good. She said it will take at least six months. I told her I could handle that.

So, we were beginning the process of packing up and putting things in storage to move out. Welch was supportive. It was not about keeping up with the Jones, I mean trying to keep the house. I had put a lot of money in this house. I worked hard to keep it. I wanted a house for my children. I wanted something better for my children. It took so long for us to move because I was trying to work it out with the bank and loan company. But the way Howard had tied up the house in the end legally there was nothing I could do. So, I lost the war and had to move.

## Chapter 13

The next month was a difficult adjustment. My grandmother was a little impatient; I had to constantly remind her the move was temporary. I know I had some of my family constantly undermining me. Keith Brown said in his book Chitilins "All family is not family". I knew what he meant now. But we were okay- I paid half of the bills. I made every attempt to keep the kids out of her way. Michael and I continued to see each other. We begin to have spontaneous sex. It didn't matter. If we felt like it, we stopped and acted like teenagers. We might go down a dirt road and park. I didn't know the fear of getting caught. It was just a rush. It really made sense not to spend money on a hotel because we were not able to spend the whole night. At 40 years old my grandmother had given me a curfew. I had to be home by 1:00 am or the door would be locked. Then sometimes when I would be late I had to knock on my cousin's window so he could let me in. I remember Welch and I were sitting in his truck. We were fooling around. She would turn on the outside light about 5 minutes till 1:00 am. It was so embarrassing. She has always been like that.

I wasn't even staying in her house when I was 21. I was staying with Lessie. She came by one Sunday Morning before she went to church. I had stayed out all night for the first time. Yes I was scared when I got home. But all I expected was a good cursing. I was grown. When I arrived home at approximately 10:00 am everyone was gone to church except my brother, David. I went in my room. My mattress was gone. I checked my closet-my clothes were gone. David said you need to check the car. I went to my window and looked. All my stuff was in my car and the mattress was on top. He said you need to read the note. I said what note. He said it's laying on what is left of your bed. I picked it up and read it. The note said "Put that shit back in the house and bring your ass to church".

## CAN'T LET GO PART ONE

I threw the note down and sat on the box spring. I said I'm not going to bring nothing in the house. I didn't put it out there.

My brother knew I was being stubborn or maybe he was trying to save me. He brought everything back in the house. Then he said get your ass to church before I whip you. I didn't want to mess with him. So I went to church. When I got to church she made me sit by her. When it was time for anyone to come up for prayer, she made me go. I said to myself I didn't need prayer I need sleep. But, I was trying to please her. So, I went.

From then on, we had a real understanding-you do not stay out all night long no matter how old you were.

He talked me into it-Let's go to New Orleans. It was the 3rd weekend in March. I was glad he did. This way we could spend some quality time together. His best friend ran a tour company called Come With Us Entertainment. Their motto was "We don't trip we just tripped". Come With Us Entertainment Inc. was a tour group formed by two guys named Bobby and Calvin. They were life long best friends-then they added two more, Bobby's co-worker Barry, or B-money (B for Baller), and Calvin's nephew Darryl. They planned tour group vacations. They used a chartered bus. They solicited people to ride for a fee. The price includes the ride and motel fees. You could watch movies if you were bored. In my case I didn't know how to play chess or spades. So I played like I was interested in the movies they played. They gave out door prizes on the bus. We had spades and chess tournaments. They had alcoholic beverages for those that like to participate. The bus will take you around the city so you don't have to worry about cab and bus fees. If you have any problems you find them. They were your host.

Now don't get twisted-this was not a swinger's trip. I know your mind was reading more into what you just read. It was good clean fun among grown folks. But one of the mottos was what happens on the bus stays on the bus. On the last night in the city they planned a little thank you party just to show their appreciation.

I have never gone on a trip away with a man. If I did the kids were there. So I was nervous. I had to save my money-I borrowed some party outfits from my best friend Maxine. Maxine had a wardrobe out of this world. She was mother of two-she was the sassy one in the M-Connection. Her husband was always letting her shop. So, when she buys something she didn't like, I got all her hand me downs. Besides, I knew I would never go anywhere to wear them again. She just likes to shop. So why spend unnecessary money?

All my friends were encouraging me to get away. If only they knew my secret. They would say you need to live. Get out of Williamsville. What better place than New Orleans to get your freak on.

Thursday night at 11:30 pm., we met in the parking lot of Kmart in Macon. He introduced me to everyone. I got on the bus and found a seat by the window. I brought a blanket and a pillow, so I could be comfortable. It was going to be a long ride. I knew they would freeze me to death with the air conditioner, so I came prepared. He put his things across from me. He went around socializing with everyone he knew. I sat nervously and peacefully. I did not know anyone. I was scared to death that his wife may drive up and show out. I know you are saying she should catch your ass and stomp it. As the bus began to leave, I said ok Lord, I know I'm wrong but please let me come back home to my children in one piece.

As he sat across from me, we pretended to be strangers. I guess making sure the people on the bus didn't know he had a wife. Apparently, he was safe. I was having a conversation with this lady sitting behind me; she was questioning me on the book I was reading. We were having a good conversation, but he felt the need to butt in from time to time. When that wasn't good enough he got up and sat next to me. Our conversation continued, but then I felt his hand under my blanket. He was rubbing my spot, my right breast, I was getting hot. All the while he was doing that, I was trying to appear normal. I didn't want her to know he was getting me aroused.

Finally another member on the bus called her and got her attention. By this time his hand had found his way between my legs. He whispered this is going to be a weekend to remember. At this time the lady leaned up and asked are you all a couple. He said yes. She said I should have known. You all look lovely together.

That was the longest ride ever; don't get me wrong-I had fun. I met new people with the same interests. We were all getting along good.

But he kept playing with me. He would fondle and tease me every chance he got. I was like a volcano ready to erupt. Anticipation had set in.

When we made it to New Orleans, I wanted to ask him if we were going to share the same room, but I didn't want to sound anxious. But when they passed out room keys, I noticed that our room keys didn't match. I got a little pissed and thought I hope I'm not sharing a room with some loud mouth, snoring and stuck up woman. I hate sidity/uppity people. Everything they got or do is better than you. They got a better story than you. So I took a deep breath. He said wait in the lobby until we get everything off the bus. I acted like I was a good wife and did as I was told. No one questioned me about sharing a room with me. I thought, well. I will have a nice room to myself. Then I smiled to myself and thought maybe Michael can sneak in late at night for some good sex.

He told me my room was on the 14th floor and I could go ahead. He needed to help them unload. So the bellhop helped me with my things and escorted me upstairs. All the way upstairs, I prayed for a miracle-maybe he'll be in the room waiting for me. I opened the door-nothing. No champagne, wine glasses, roses, or lover were present. So I unpacked and put my things away. We were supposed to meet the group downstairs at 4:00 pm. I got my things laid out so I could take a good hot bath and a nap. They had a lot of things planned for the evening. I let the water run with Bath and Body Works Strawberry Bubble Bath Oil. I had bubbles everywhere. I stepped in. I let my mind drift away. But I heard something that brought me back to reality; there he was standing there like a light skinned Amazon. I said what are you doing here and how did you get in. He said I told you this was going to be a weekend to remember.

He stepped in and pulled me close to him. He asked me to stand up. He wanted to see my body wet. As the water ran down my body, he said please don't let anyone mess with my stuff. I said who am I gonna give it to. You got it on lock down. He said well. We bathed one another. As we stood up, he turned me around and entered into me. It seemed as if we could not get enough of each other. We went on forever. I heard the phone ring, by that time I was sitting on top of him-riding. He was sucking on my titties. I know I wasn't gonna stop to answer the phone. Then we heard someone knocking like the hotel was on fire. We kept at it. The bath water was cold. So we stood up and took a shower together. As we dried off he looked at me. I said what. He picked me up and put me on the sink. He placed my legs on his shoulder. He began to love me as if I were the only one in his life. He couldn't stop. He asked who this belong to? I said yours. While breathing heavily, he would say don't you give this to anyone else. This belongs to me. I will do right by you. When he finished we had to take another shower. In the end we finally had to heed the knocking. While we were drying off I told him I'll dry off in the room you stay in here. I said we will never leave if we keep this up.

I wondered what time it was. He said let me check. It was 3:40 pm. I said Oh my God we are going to be late. He said that's good. We can spend our time alone. But I knew his best friend was not gonna allow us that opportunity. He was ready to party. So we got dressed and hurried downstairs.

Once we reached downstairs the majority of the group was present. They were staring at us like they knew we been doing the nasty. I didn't care. If they didn't have someone to get their groove on with that was none of my business just like it was none of their business what I was doing upstairs.

When you have a large group they can not agree on what to do. Most don't have the money to operate with and do the things they want to and they just be trying to impress the next man. So I let them know up front I'm cheap and living on a budget.

Now we had a bus to use but the bus drivers said they were tired, which was understandable. So we rented two vans to go down to Bourbon Street. Once we reached there we would split up. I said to myself thank you, Michael; I don't have to be bothered with people who we don't know. It was nice and warm for the month of March. It was crowded. Mardi Gras had been a few weeks prior. People were everywhere.

Now, I know what they mean when they say you can put your hair down. Everything you could want was in one place. The French Quarter, River Walk, casinos, hotels, restaurants, the Cavern New Orleans, and clubs, there was even a flea market. Michael and I decided to try out the casinos. I had made my mind up to spend only ten dollars, win or lose. As we moved around to different games and I slowly lost my money I watched in amazement at the types of people in the casino. It was amazing to see the old people in the casino; some looked as if they were dirt poor. One of the waitresses said this is their way of living. They come here and take a chance at winning everyday. I thought that was sad. Once in a while someone would hit the jackpot, but I wondered how much they put in the pot. It wasn't anyone who looked poor that won.

Welch and I finally decided to call it quits. We walked outside to wait on the others that were with us. That's when Welch realized he had lost his wallet. He quickly ran back inside to where we were sitting and playing games. A couple of the guys that were with us went in with him to help.

Finally, Welch came back and said someone had turned his wallet into the lost and found, but they had taken all his money. But they didn't take his checkbook. I know it sounded a little fishy. But, I went along with him, because he was going to find out I don't play about my money and I had already been used one time. I asked him did he want to check around with some places that can cash a check for him. He said yes. But without transportation due to someone wanting the van, us really not knowing the city, and the late hour, we decided to do it in the morning. Jeff offered to loan him some money before I did.

So it worked out. Michael and I were friends and lovers but those dead presidents and I have a bond. It was till death do us part and since they were already dead I promised to stay with them until I die. I told Michael we can find a check cashing place to cash his check in the morning, and I would help him out if he needed it-he just needed to pay me back. He agreed.

The last night after the party at the Hilton, we all decided to go to this club called 360-Three Hundred Sixty Degrees. It was on the 30th Floor of the Moroccan Building. It overlooked the Mississippi River and New Orleans. It gradually spins around. Architects are genius. So you can sit at the bar and view everything.

When I thought everything was perfect, you know someone had to show out. One of the members, Darryl, and his girlfriend got into an argument. She apparently caught him making eyes at one of the ladies that came on the trip. After making a scene, she left. Nobody wanted to follow her because we didn't know what kind of mind frame she was in. But finally I was being brave and said we need to find her. I said this is a big city and I don't want anything to happen. Welch said her ass should not have left. I elbowed him in his side and gave him that look.

So, we all proceeded to leave and find her. Welch, Bobby and I walked, while the others used the van. Even though we were looking for her, we had a beautiful walk back to the hotel. When we arrived at the hotel-she had left a message for us at the front desk. It said I do not want to be fucked with until the morning. Everyone else was mad, me I was glad she was alright and I can enjoy my evening.

We all stayed up late playing spades and eating pizza. But I was ready for something else. We made an excuse to leave. Once we got on the elevator, he pushed the stop button and we made love right there. He kneeled down and lifted my dress up. I had on a short mini dress with a thong. So, he didn't have much work to do. He began to taste me right there. After we finished, we laughed like kids and pushed the elevator button to go. When we arrived on our floor and the door opened, we peeped out to see if security was waiting for us. We didn't see anyone. So, we made a mad dash to our room.

Once in the room, we took a long shower together. Once we lay in the bed, we both fell into a deep sleep. Tomorrow, we will return back to reality. We will return home.

## Chapter 14

I returned from the trip feeling revived. I kept hearing those words in my ears: I will do right by you. Those words that he whispered to me while holding me during one of our lovemaking sessions. I had hope. I felt that maybe I wasn't being made a fool of. He wanted me. I prayed he wasn't lying.

When I came in to work, one of my associates Ms. Thomas pulled me to the side. She said you know they swapped out all the supervisors. I said why. Ms. Reese is on the warpath. I asked who are we getting. She said Sgt. Blair, Lt. Salsa, Sgt. Bolton, and Sgt. Edwards. I said oh I don't have a problem with them. She said yes you do. I said I do? She said you just don't know it yet. She said I will call you when you get home just give me your home phone number. I didn't want her to have it. It will be breaking one of my rules: socializing with coworkers after hours. I gave her my phone number anyway.

After waiting all day, she called me. She said I know you don't want anybody to know that you and Counselor Welch are dating, so I will pretend that I don't know you all are. She said this information that I'm gonna give you may not apply to you. Since, you don't go with him. I said I guess not but tell me anyway. She said you know Sgt. Blair and Mr. Welch was an item when he worked there earlier in his career. I said get out-she said yeah. She said the street committee said you and him are going to respect her when she comes on shift. I said ain't she married? She said yeah. She said the word is he knew better than to come back out there to work and disrespect her especially with you. I said with me? I said it before I knew it, she ain't all that. Who does she think she is?

I knew then I was really Dorothy of the Wizard of OZ. Because I woke up then; the wicked witch of the east showed up.

You see Ms. Thomas knows everything and everybody. If you need to know the 411, she has it. She was better than a 24 hour weather channel. So, more than likely the information was true.

From the first day I worked with this particular supervisor, Sgt. Blair, we had tension. I mean we were not feeling each other. She always went for bad. She had this evil demeanor. As if someone was going to let her beat their ass. Women that are a little thick think they can handle small women. See, if you're small you have to use other means to handle large subjects, if you know what I mean. So since I wasn't feeling her I stayed out of her way. She was not worth me losing my job. Now if I still worked at the factory that would be another thing. Back then you could fight and they gave you the rest of the day off and you can come back to work the next day. Just like she thought she had it going on, I thought I did too. I wasn't gonna let any one run over me even if she had rank.

We all know people that get a little rank who don't need it. They lack personality. They know the job but they are not a people person. The first day on my shift her sidekick, Sgt. May and her got on their brooms and went to interrogate Welch in his office in the Education Building. He would come in at 8:00. They would make their rounds at 8:20. It didn't bother me. I was worried about the street committee and what they would be saying. I couldn't help but wonder if you are over with someone why would you be in their face. If you're married and say you are happy why jeopardize your home.

I guess she couldn't get any information from him about me. She sent out the search parties. Remember those ugly monkeys in the Wizard of Oz. One of them had the nerve to ask me point blank-are you seeing Counselor Welch. I looked at her and I should have said that was none of your business. But I had to be professional; I said no we were good friends, besides how could anyone go with a married man. Yes, I was lying. She said Oh you know he's married. I said yes. She said didn't you go to New Orleans with him. I said no I went to New Orleans by myself. I said ain't you being personal. She said no girl you know I thought we were cool like that. I said yeah I did too. I asked her how was her husband was doing. The street committee said he was doing drugs and couldn't keep a job. That's how you kill those monkeys-you got to flip the conversation. She said we are doing good,

I'll tell him you asked about him. She walked off.

## Chapter 15

While, I had drama going on at work, home was getting worse. The only time they give you credit is when one of your children messes up. I had my second sign from God-I could not put my finger on it but I knew something was wrong. My baby, my little girl, was only 11. Her behavior changed-she had an attitude. She was so quick to get too angry. Grades weren't so good. Every chance she got she didn't want to stay home; she wanted to stay at my mother's. My mother's house was like the YMCA. Every boy and girl in the neighborhood was in and out of my mother's house.

I should have seen it coming. But between working, 4 kids, their activities, my housing situation, and don't let me forget about him, I was not stable. It's as if when it comes to him I got side tracked. The world slowed down. But I knew I could trust my children. I did not expect one of my children to disappoint me so horribly this soon. We talked about everything openly-sex, drugs, peer pressure, and any problems. I kept an open door policy with them. I demanded that they tell me first before someone else tells me no matter how bad it is.

So one night, after spending time with Michael, it happens. I walked in my room. I saw a letter on my pillow. I knew it was from Cameron. He loves leaving me little notes telling on someone. He doesn't have the guts to do it in person. I guess he really feared the demons in me. I think he hadn't forgotten when he had seen me in that state before. The note read Momma, Kira went out of the house. When she came back she had leaves on her, and then she went straight to the bathroom. I was wandering what in the hell was he talking about.

See I have names for my children. I have the FBI who is Cameron. He tells you what you need to know case by case or when it's beneficial for him. I have the CIA who is Sean. If you don't ask he is not gonna tell. He said he didn't have anything to do with it. It wasn't his business. Then I have the GBI-Kira. She tells on everybody and everyone, but herself. She doesn't discriminate how big or little the incident. She will tell. Then last but not least, the IRS, Josh, he keeps account of everything. His mind is like a computer, he does not forget anything. I was blessed when he graduated-he went right into the Air Force.

All kinds of thoughts were running through my mind. I called Cameron into my room and asked him what he was talking about. He said Kira had been sneaking out of the house. He said she had been meeting this boy. I said do what. He said she been going out of grandma's house-she stays out for a while-when she comes back-she goes into the bathroom and runs the water. He said I asked her what she had been doing-she cursed me out and said mind your damn business. I asked Cameron why didn't you tell me before. I had to get my facts straight, he said. I thought to myself just like the FBI. When they tell you something the damage already been done. He said I believe she was getting booty. I said yeah.

I was furious. I wanted to choke her. So I calmed down because I didn't want to wake up my grandmother. I walked in her room. I looked at her and thought, not my little baby-I'll kill him, no I'll cut his dick off then I'll kill him then I'll kill her. I woke her up. She acted so sleepy. I asked her to come in my room. I made Cameron stay in my room since he was a witness. He may need to testify. I know he wanted to stay; he wanted to see the sentencing part.

My motto in my courtroom is you are guilty until proven innocent. So, there was no need to be sworn in. If you lie that is worse than the actual act itself. So it's in your best interest to tell the truth.

I wasn't gonna wait until the morning to have court. We were having night court at 11:15 pm. She came in my room. I asked her have you been having sex. She said no mommy what are you talking about. I heard Cameron say Humph. I told Cameron to shut up. Kira said Cameron's just lying because I told on him. I haven't done anything. I asked her how did you get leaves on you. She said I was running from grandma's house to Lessie's house and fell. That's how I got leaves on me. She looks and sounds so convincing, I said to myself, looking like Clarence Thomas knowing he fucked Anita Hill and got away with it. I knew she was guilty of something, I hoped it wasn't that.

If you had a childhood, most kids experiment with sex. When I was growing up we called it hunching. You never take your clothes off. We thought it was alright because you could not see the private parts. This generation changed it-you got to take your clothes off and teenage pregnancy was up. People constantly debated when to put your daughter on birth control pills. Some say as soon as possible. Some say no if you put them on it that's giving them the okay. Some say I am not putting them on anything. Nobody put me on pills, I didn't get pregnant. Lessie told us if we got pregnant we were quitting school and getting a job where she worked. My mother worked at a factory, when she came home she had cotton all over her. She looked like a snowman all year long. She had cotton everywhere, even up her nose. It was a living, but I was not planning on getting a job there. I was too cute.

So, I took it all in and said well you don't have a problem if I take you to the hospital in the morning. That way they can check you out. They will be able to tell me if you had sex or not. That confident look she had slowly went away. I said you know how I feel about lying. If you are lying I will put you in the YDC after we leave the hospital. You know I'll do it too. So you need to tell the truth now. Cameron slowly moved away from me. He didn't want to be close in case he had to duck.

It took her a minute before she broke, I really didn't want to hear it. But I had to know. Because if it's something I need to fix, I'll fix it.

Finally she said yeah. I said say that again. She said yes. I asked her with who. She said Deontae and Rascal. I could not believe what I was hearing. I said do you know what you were doing? You know you can catch aids and get pregnant. She said they used condoms. That scratched out my theory they were just hunching with their clothes on. I wanted to slap her, but I knew she would run and cry. It would wake up my grandmother.

I said you are too young. I said; hold up you said with Deontae and Rascal? I asked how many times have you done it? She said 3 with Deontae and 1 time with Rascal. I said have you lost your mind? It was after 12:00 then. I said is there anyone else. I got up and started pacing. By that time Cameron had made it out of the room. Kira was in the doorway looking like she was ready to run.

I called a family meeting. The kids and I sit and discuss the event whether it was good or bad. Especially, if it's going to affect someone in the family, we need to talk about it. I had to decide whether to press charges on the boys who were 15. All our families were so close. As we discussed the matter, I noticed Kira didn't seem remorseful. That's when I decided for her to take us to the spot. I asked where was the act committed.

Once we arrived there, it was a patch of bushes no more that 25 feet from the house. I broke me off a switch and whipped her behind right there. Once I was finished, I made Cameron and Sean go back to the house. I made Kira take her clothes off. She took them off. I asked do you feel shamed and humiliated. She said yes as she started crying. I said see he didn't respect you. I said animals have sex on the ground not humans.

As she stood there she said I'm cold. I said you weren't cold when you were doing it. I told her you will always remember this was how you lost your virginity. She said I feel nasty. I said I know you do. She sat on the ground and cried more. I let her put her clothes on. I told her I was going to press charges. She said it was her fault I wanted to do it and they didn't make me do it. I said what. My friends were doing it. She said Mommy I don't want nobody to know-please don't say anything. I had a lot to think about. Because the way she explained it, they should all be locked up.

So, I told her we'll talk later. On Sunday we all went to church. On Monday, I took her to the doctor who also was a good friend. Kira knew her so she felt comfortable when she was examined. She said Kira didn't contract any STD nor was she pregnant. I also scheduled Kira some counseling with the Clinical Psychiatrist.

I knew I had to tell someone what had happened or I would have a nervous breakdown. So when Welch called I confided in him. Since he was a counselor he said he would talk to Kira too. I told him that I will be cutting the amount of time that we were spending together. I can't afford to lose my child. He understood. The kids and I began to have family meetings, weekly. I agreed not to press charges but I made a visit to their parents. They were very happy I didn't press charges but they will deal with their sons on their level. I told them there will not be a second chance.

# Chapter 16

I was recovering from the incident with Kira. I found myself wanting to be at work. I didn't want to stay at home. I was fine as long as the kids were there, but I didn't want to be reminded about Kira's sexual activity. When I was alone I thought about how it was my fault all the time, even though I knew I couldn't be with them all the time. I just have to pray harder they are doing right.

I was always late for work-even if I get there on time, I would play around in the car or walk slow. But the last month, I have been getting close calls. I hit a deer; thankfully it didn't damage my car. But it scared the daylights out of me. I noticed I started to see more deer. One morning I hit the brakes and I almost slid in the ditch. So, I started leaving home for work earlier. Welch would call me to make sure I was up. He was considerate that way.

This particular morning, it had rained so I left earlier. The stretch to work is a lot of back roads. I was listening to my radio thinking about Welch. See, I have driven practically all over the state and never had a wreck or fender bender. So I was confident in my driving.

It was lightly raining, water was standing in the road and I was coming up to a curve. I knew better than to hit the brakes. I have given people advice on handling their car when it begins to hydroplane. But what do I do, I hit my brakes. The car begins to cross the road sideways. I tried to turn it, but it wouldn't turn. I tried pumping the brakes-it got worse. But then I remembered to let the car go with it, don't snatch the steering wheel. I just prayed not to hit a tree head on.

As the car was gliding toward the trees, I knew I didn't want to die. Even though I would be talking that shit to the inmates. I would say I'm not afraid to die. I'm ready to go whenever the Lord is ready. Knowing good and damn well I was lying. I leaned over into the passenger seat, I didn't want to see what was gonna happen next. I asked the Lord please don't take me from Josh, Cameron, Sean and Kira. I'm not ready to go now. They need me.

It felt like the car was spinning, somewhat like flying. Finally the car stopped-I sat up. All I could see was darkness, I smelled gas. I tried to open my door. It wouldn't budge. My air bag didn't come out so I thought it can't be that bad. Then I said to myself I need to get out before this car blows up, so I tried my door again. I still couldn't open it. I looked over at the passenger side and saw that the window was broken out.

It was still dark. I found my cell phone and purse. I crawled out the passenger window. I hit the ground. My purse fell out of my hand so I crawled around in the wet grass looking for it. I was getting upset about my uniform. I probably had gotten it soiled from the ground and I had just gotten it out of the cleaners. I found my purse. It had my income tax refund check in it. I was relieved. I ran up the road as far as I could. I stopped and checked myself. I didn't feel hurt. I didn't feel any blood. I didn't have any broken bones. I seemed to be alright. So I pulled my cell phone out of my purse to see did I have a signal.

I thought I need to call the prison and tell them I was late. I knew I should have been calling an ambulance or the police or I should have fallen on my knees and prayed. After walking back and forth trying to get a signal acting like the man on the Verizon Wireless commercial, I finally got one. He needs to walk in the woods next time he does that commercial and see can someone hear him. Nobody will hear him but the snakes and the deer. I finally got my supervisor. I asked could she send someone to pick me up. I told her my car was in the ditch. I didn't need her to be alarmed so I acted calm. I told her I was alright. I could hear Sgt. Dixon with her big mouth self in the background where is Froony at. That was my nickname she gave me. So I explained to her my location.

It seemed like forever until I finally saw some headlights coming toward my direction. I knew it couldn't be her because the prison wasn't that way. So I stepped off the road because I didn't want to be on Missing Persons. But the car slowed down by my car and then it turned around. I saw it positioning itself with the headlights aimed at my car. I hoped they would call for help. I had a good view of my vehicle. I couldn't believe it. I said I tore that car up.

So, then I heard someone calling my name. It was Sgt. Dixon. She was just yelling my name. Sgt Dixon was a round short butterball woman but she had a beautiful face. She was a good spirited person. But she cursed like a wino after he had spent all of his SSI check on liquor and got drunk.

I yelled out to her here I am I could hear her just a cursing. She said where in the hell are you at. Girl is your god damn ass alright she said as if she was in a panic. Froony you done tore this m……..f……..g car up. How you gonna say you are in the ditch when your ass done been hang gliding in this bitch. I couldn't get a word in as she went on and on. Believe it or not she hadn't taken but one breath. Finally, when she hesitated, I told her I hydroplaned. She said No hell you didn't-your ass played demolition derby and lost against them trees.

When she couldn't curse anymore she called to the prison and told the lead supervisor. I had to hear the whole sermon again. I heard her say she looked alright but she needs psychological help this Bitch walking around like she alright. Something is wrong with her ass, she said she don't know she could have been dead. So I told her I had a headache so she would stop talking so loud.

As daybreak came up, we could see my car. I got out and walked around it. I could not believe the damage. Everyone that rode by stopped and asked did the person make it. They were talking like I wasn't standing there. Someone asked who was driving. I thought maybe I died and just hadn't crossed over. I could hear them say there is no way she is still alive. Some just shook their head and looked shocked. When they found out it was me, they said the Lord was with you. You must be living right.

The State Trooper walked up and said you hit eight trees. The car spun around twice. The bigger trees left impressions in my rear driver side door and at the front of the gas tank. Two trees hit the front of the car at an angle. The trunk was pushed into the back seat. He said your personal assets that were in the trunk were thrown 20 feet into the woods. In the end, he gave me a ticket for driving too fast for the conditions. I said I wasn't speeding. Then my head was hurting for real. I said to myself I'm not trying to argue about a ticket, am I? I could be arguing with St. Peter an hour ago if the Lord had not spared my life.

Then, Sgt. Dixon encouraged me to ride in the ambulance. I agreed-I didn't need her cursing me out all the way to the hospital. She followed though. She told me you know your stupid ass was walking the wrong direction, the prison was that way. She said I thought you needed to know and closed the ambulance door. See she can curse me like that because we cursed each other like that. Nobody else can get away with that.

As I rode to the hospital, I wondered did anyone tell him yet. How was he gonna react? Would he show up at the hospital and hold my hand? Surely at least he would call. I didn't hear anything.

Sgt. Dixon had contacted my mother. She said she was coming. I told her to make sure that she tells her I was alright. After I was examined and they found nothing was wrong with me the nurse said I can go home. She gave me a prescription for pain. Sgt. Dixon asks the Doctor can they examine my brain. She told him I was a mental health case.

Lessie arrived as we sat in the lobby. I knew when we left the hospital she wanted to fuss. But, she didn't say anything except they got the kids out of school and they were home. They didn't want to risk someone calling the school and telling them. I wish she had of fussed and got it over with. When I was released and made it home everyone was being nosey. The kids looked at me when I walked through the door. They just sat there and looked at me. Finally, Sean said ain't nothing wrong with you can I go back to school. He said I don't want to miss my game. I said yes you can. I kept telling everyone who called my cell phone I was alright. The kids gave me a hug. I had Lessie take them back to school. I never want them to worry about me.

I checked the house phone and my cell phone every chance I got. He still didn't call. Finally around 3:00 he called. He said you know everyone was being nosey, that's why I didn't come. I really wanted to come he said. He explained he had class. I allowed myself to understand. He said he would call me when he got off work. I said call, you mean you are not gonna come see me? He said not today I know you don't want to risk some of the coworkers seeing me. I said you weren't worried before if they knew, is it because your ex is working this shift? I said your ass has been acting funny every since she hit daylight at work.

He said no I haven't. I said you told me you loved me. Before he could respond I hung up and turned the ringer off.

## Chapter 17

I was still bitter because he didn't come to see me when I had the accident. I had to constantly remind myself-McKenzie, he is married. But I gave myself to him, he wanted to go public, not me. My family was sitting idlely by not saying a word but wanting to say something. I know Lessie would say what good is he if he doesn't come when you need him.

Since, I wasn't seriously hurt from the car accident I returned to work in a couple of days. It was like an evangelist preacher had poured anointment oil over my body, said you are healed and no weapon formed will prosper against you but you got to do right. It was a miracle. I lied to the Lord that I was gonna end it with him, again. The Lord had spared my life. Too many bad things were happening to me.

The insurance company paid off the car with enough for a down payment for another car. I talked to my bank. Ms. Black the vice-president said go find you a car, we will finance it. My mother could not understand how I did it. See, as you may know, if you have a good history with your bank, they will take care of you. The house didn't show up on my credit report. My credit report looks as if I didn't buy a house. I went to my bank and was honest. I told them the truth. Since the Lord and Honda Accord Ex spared my life, I went and bought a new Navy Blue Honda Accord Ex which was fully loaded. I drove it in the yard. Nobody came out to look at it. Lessie had told my grandmother that there was no way I was gonna get another car. She told her she just lost a house and her credit was jacked up how was she gonna get a new car. As usual, my grandmother always kept me informed. I told her I was gonna get the kind of car I want and at the price I want.

Black people always blamed the white people for their downfalls. I can't do that. On my first job the owner, who was white, came up to me and said you are too smart to be here you need to go to college.

At this time I was pregnant so when I went out on maternity leave he let me file for unemployment. All the way through school I drew unemployment and welfare benefits. I was able to get into all kinds of programs because I was in school. I had the baby and enrolled at a Technical College taking Accounting. I graduated with honors. A white person got me a job with the government. So far I have been with them 20 years. Each time I transferred to get closer to home or get a promotion it was a white person that helped me. A white person gave me a loan without a cosigner. So, yes, we hold ourselves back. We have to keep knocking at doors until we find the right ones that will open.

Again, I talked to Welch about us not seeing each other so much. Or maybe I needed to see someone else. I told him I realized we didn't have a future. He said what if I wanted to marry you. I said how you gonna say that when you haven't even got a divorce. I looked at him and said you really think I'm stupid. He said I'm not ready to lose you. I asked why are you holding on to me. You know you are not doing me any good. He told me about a trip coming up in Daytona, and asked me to go. He said I'm gonna have a big surprise for you. I made excuses. I said my money wasn't right and I need a babysitter. He said please try to go, please don't disappoint me. I said I just don't know.

Finally, I stood firm and said no I'm not going. At least I thought I was firm. He was trying everything possible to have his cake and eat it too.

As the month went by, he kept begging and hinting about the surprise. Kira was doing better. She slept with me at night. Sometimes she cried in her sleep. The counseling really helps her. I turned down nights out with Welch. I needed to be a mother again. The mother my children knew and loved. Besides I can be a woman when they become grown. I've got time. But they need me now. She told me Momma I didn't mean to make you cry. I said I need to cry. I needed to be reminded I am a mother first. I told her you are a smart and beautiful girl-you just made a bad choice. It is over now just don't do it again. She said I won't-anyway I have been re-born again. I said what is re-born? She said I have claimed what happened is in the past and I am a virgin again to the Lord. As she went to sleep, she said I love you. I said I love you too.

The weekend of Mother's Day was always busy. We were planning a cookout for my grandmother-all the kids and grandkids were going to be attending. Welch had let me know earlier he would be going out of town to his mother's house.

Sunday morning my children were up bright and early cooking breakfast for me. They cooked pancakes, bacon and eggs. They also had my favorite Tropicana Orange Juice (not from concentrate). They brought everything to my room. I told them I can't eat in here and Momma will kill me. They said no she won't she has gone to church, already. Then they all went to laughing.

After I finished eating, they each brought me a Mother's Day Card they had made. Then they brought me one that they had paid for. I asked where did you all get the money from. They said don't worry about that. Then they gave me a box. A small jewelry box was placed in my hand. I said what is this? By the time I got it open they gave me the phone-it was Michael. He said Happy Mother's Day. Tears came to my eyes. The children and he had given me a heart shaped diamond pendant necklace. It was beautiful. Michael said do you like it? I said yes. I said thank you. I didn't want to spoil the moment, since the children were in on the gift.

But he knew we needed to talk. He knew I was trying to end it. He said there is more in Daytona. He had won my children over. The kids were egging me on-Momma go to Daytona we will take care of Kira. They said nobody will get in trouble-they promised. I agreed to go Daytona.

## Chapter 18

The next weekend, I made final preparations to go to Daytona. He better tell me he's getting a divorce. My Grandmother gave me the go ahead. She really liked Michael Welch.

She probably liked any man that would get me out of her house. I lined her pocket with money, so she will not fuss at me too bad. Daytona was a short trip. 6 hours and we were entering the hotel. This was a 3 day trip. We left on Friday at 8:00 am and will be back on Sunday evening. We acted as we were still the perfect couple. The majority of the tourists had gone on the previous trip. So they all knew us. They would ask me where is your shadow. It was a reunion. This time I was more relaxed. I made up my mind if he doesn't present any divorce papers, when we get off this bus it is over.

When we arrived in Daytona, we shared rooms again. We christened the room by making love in both beds. We stayed on the 14th floor overlooking the Daytona Beach. He knew how I loved God's creation. I loved watching the sun go up and down. How the sky changed colors. I had my children looking at the sky when we go places. I would tell them Man can mess with a lot of things but they can't mess with the sun and the sky.

After getting our freak on, we decided to go walking. First we walked down the strips and looked around the tour shops. I don't know what is the big deal about going shopping in another state. They have the same thing in every state. If I were rich, I would feel the same way. Besides that I hate shopping and spending unnecessary money.

My sisters and I (my biological sisters by Lessie, Victoria and Faith) went shopping in the Galleria Mall in Macon. We had our first family moment. We have not had one since we were grown. My middle sister (Victoria) was always teasing me about how tight I was about spending money. As we were walking she said you hear that. We said what.

She said that squeaking noise. We said no. She went to laughing and said to me, McKenzie when you walk you squeak, that's how tight on spending money you are. We all laughed out loud, because she was telling the truth.

Welch and I always held hands when we walked together. We didn't care if people were looking. We were just that way. As we talked face to face we used a lot of eye contact. We ended up on the beach as the sun was going down. I said this would be the perfect moment to give me my surprise. But instead we found a good place to be intimate.

I had on a black wrap skirt so all we had to do was lift it up. So I slid my panties to the side and he stood behind me. We made love while the sun was going down. When we finished he said let's hurry up we are going to miss dinner. I thought well maybe this will be it.

Before dinner I decided to call home and check on the kids. My grandma said Cameron had gone to the emergency room for his arm. But nothing was broken. They just put it in a sling. I asked her did he hurt it in practice. She said no. It took her a while; finally she said he was with my cousin. She said Cameron was sitting in the back seat. He pulled out in front of someone and the car hit his side of the car. She said he was alright and not to worry. She said no need to come home. I said where is Cameron? She said outside playing. She said don't worry. I said OK; tell the children I love them. She said OK and hung up. I sat down in the lobby and prayed a little prayer.

I went upstairs and informed Michael of what had happened. He said what else is gonna happen and you know I'm gonna be there for you no matter what happens. I said to myself, you're probably the reason everything's been happening.

We went out to eat-still no surprise. We went dancing-still no surprise. I was getting a little angry by this time. So when we got back to the hotel and we were drinking some white wine, I asked Michael what kind of surprise do you have for me. He said I got a transfer. I said where. He said to Williamsville State Prison-see, I can see you everyday.

This prison was in my home town. He said I will be doing the same thing. I said you know Howard works there don't you. He said he'll be alright. I said OK. I said this was the surprise? He said yes, what did you think it was? I said nothing. I told him I was happy for him. He said now I don't have to put up with Sgt. Blair meddling in our business. I said yes you are right about that-she will be meddling with me now.

I wandered how Howard was going to take the news-my boyfriend will be working with him. Howard thought he owned that prison.

The next day Michael went out on the beach with Bobby for a swim. I took it upon myself to do a shakedown through his suitcases. I didn't find an engagement ring or any separation/divorce papers. I just hoped there was more to the surprise. I sat on the balcony and watched them act like five year old boys. I didn't want to lose him. I still wanted to be in his life. I do want a relationship. But I want one that is right through the eyes of the Lord. We could be friends and not have sex until he gets his situation together. I could do without sex if need be. If he's going to sacrifice and transfer to be near me then he must be serious about me. I decided to present my case to him.

I played another hand. That night after making love, we were cuddling and I said, you know this year's been rough. I could hear the cars below honking. We left the balcony doors and curtains open while we slept. So, when I woke up in the morning I could see the sun rise. I continued, I really appreciate that you have been a friend but I believe I'm going through this because you are married. He listened in silence. He said what's wrong. I said I'm not ending the relationship but I want to be friends without sex. At least until you handle your situation. He said you know we will always be friends to the end and I'm working on it. I said I know. But I can't take another disaster. He said I'll take care of it. We hugged and went to sleep. At least he did.

# Chapter 19

Michael was so excited. He could hardly wait. I gave him all types of advice. I mean really I was giving him warning signs. I hoped he would listen to me. In the past, I had worked at Williamsville State Prison for five years. So I knew the ins and outs of the work place. Majority of the people I knew there go through some type of interdepartmental relationship or at least is affected by one.

I told him don't do the following: 1) don't drink the water-When you drink the water people tends to see somebody that look better than the one they have at home. When you get the new person home with you-you realize they are similar to the one you got rid of. I called these kinds of people Artificial Turf. There is an old saying the grass looks greener on the other side. That kind of grass is Artificial Turf. It's green, pretty, and healthy looking.

Artificial Turf is pretty, but it is also fake and phony. If you lift it up, it has weeds underneath. That's like when people take off their makeup, and pull the weave out their hair, and wears those fake Lee Press On Nails. Don't let me forget those different kinds of cheap oils that smell good for thirty minutes, after they are put on. When you take all of it off, that's a rough looking individual.

People forget it costs a lot to maintain that look. Then you find out they are maxxed out on all those credit cards they have. Majority of everyone fixes up to go to work. It is part of their self esteem and hygiene. But, there are a few that do it to look for a man. But when you get them home with you-you see the true side. Especially, in the morning- you take a long look at them after a long night. Ms. Reese, my Superintendent, would say don't get your money and your honey in the same place. We would laugh at her. But, I knew what she was talking about.

2) Williamsville State Prison is Peyton Place. You have a lot of super

visitors/officers relationships. This is when the supervisors let them be off when they want to be and they get all holidays off. If that don't do it when a couple breaks up they move on to another partner like it was nothing. Better yet when the relationship doesn't go their way, they run to the front office, crying. The whole while, they were participating willingly.

3) There is an underground group that works out there-they are called the street committee (they really don't participate they just gossip). As officers you are supposed to monitor inmates-the street committee monitors the when and where of other staff members. If you visited someone's dorm for more than a minute or visited it more than one time-you are sleeping with that person.

4) Don't buy in to gossip-I had to repeat it twice to him. The street committee does not want to see some one happy. They are upset because they are really on lockdown and can't participate. The other reason nobody else wants them.

Don't get me wrong there are some good and righteous people that work there. You have to find them and make them your associates. But I guess it's depending on what kind of person you are that determines who you want to associate with.

I can tell him all of this because I had first hand experience. I had an interdepartmental relationship and I belong to the street committee. One time I was the president, I knew everything about everybody-at least I thought I did. Then another saying got me, what goes around comes around. I was caught up in the mix and got out. I could not hang. I officially resigned from the committee. That's why I had rules when I transferred to Oak Park State Prison. I do not socialize with coworkers.

I've seen people come out there happily married and ending up divorced. Then within 3 months married to someone they work with. I remember these two couples who swapped partners.

5) Last but not least-please stay away from Howard-I told him I believe Howard ran that prison. Everyone loved him .I said to him do not make any trouble for yourself. I told him again I believe Howard ran that prison.

He kept saying I got this. I knew I was talking to a brick. Because Michael Welch thinks he can do what he wants when he wants to. After being there two weeks, Howard called me and said you need to talk to your boy. I said what are you talking about. He needs to stop bragging and boasting about he is hitting you. He said you know what that is-don't you? I said yes, hitting means sex and Welch wouldn't do that. He said you don't know him very well do you. I said I'll talk to him. I asked him what does it matter to you-we are not together. He said it seems like he is trying to belittle you. I said alright. I didn't want to get into it with Howard because he thinks he is always right. But I had to ask, what is he was saying about me? Howard said he is saying yeah, me and Ms. Scott are together and how he hoped you and him will get married. I can tell Howard was pissed. Hell he was just jealous that another man finds me interesting. Howard finished by saying he talks too much and nobody wants to hear y'all's business either. I said to myself, you wouldn't want anyone out there to hear about our business.

The next week Michael came up with this idea. The prison has a pond with a picnic area. The grounds were magnificent. Those inmates took good care of those grounds. At the pond they had a little waterfall. A lot of picnic tables. They even had a walking trail for anyone who wants to get their exercise on around the pond. It was so nice. He asked me to have a picnic lunch with him by the pond. I wanted to say no. But I knew this was Michael's way of seeing if I was trying to hide our relationship from Howard. I knew Howard would think I was disrespecting him.

So, I agreed to meet Michael for lunch. I picked up our meals from the local restaurant, Nana's Kitchen. We had spaghetti dinners with lemonade. I wore a sleeveless maroon blouse with a tan pair of Capri pants, because it was so warm out. It really was warm in July. When I arrived Michael was already sitting at the picnic table wearing a white linen shirt with a pair of jeans. He was grinning as usual. He had thought of bringing a tablecloth and centerpiece for the table. It was roses, for me.

As we were finishing our meals, the perimeter car stops. The officer, who I knew, got out. I could hear a man on the radio saying who is out there. She said Counselor Welch and a friend. He said she is a state employee. I heard him say well just tell them when they finish they can't be out there. So she approached and I told her I heard the traffic on the radio. She said they called her to come and check out who was out there; they thought it was someone who didn't work here. I said yeah right. Then, she said but we were told that anyone can eat out here as long as you work for Williamsville State Prison-I really don't see the problem. But I'm not in charge. She said to me and you still work for the state. She said someone was just tripping-this is silly. I thought it didn't take a rocket scientist to figure out who that was. She left-Michael and I finished our lunch. He said that man's got problems. Michael and I stayed an extra 15 minutes over his lunch break. I knew what he was doing. He wanted to show Howard-we will leave when we get ready for us to leave. At one time, I looked up at the Prison because it sits on a hill and I saw Howard just staring at us. If looks could kill, we would be on the evening news of WMAZ Channel 13 news out of Macon. He must have seen me looking at him. He turned and walked inside swiftly.

## Chapter 20

Every so often my mother and I have to have an undercover confrontation. It is a conversation between two people that have hidden issues with each other. She always tries to find ways to push my buttons. My mother did not raise me and my sisters. She married my father and got pregnant with me. She left him while she was pregnant. After 30 years, I finally got to know him and I saw why she left him. She had my sister by another man and they broke up. She then remarried and had my baby sister. So we assumed Lessie was our sister. No one told us the history.

Back in the day there were things children shouldn't know about. Remember, when they sent you outside to play when grown people began to talk about something or gossip? I spent so much time outside. I began to think I was Tarzan. I used to pretend I was that monkey on the show.

Before she remarried she was living with us. So, when she moved out we didn't want to go. We didn't understand why she wanted us to go. Our grandparents did not want us to go, which at that time we called them momma and daddy. We called her by her first name. She didn't correct us, so she must have been fine with it.

We were raised in a family of 13. We had 7 brothers and 6 sisters including Victoria and I, Lessie being the oldest. As you see it was a large family. You know we had some good and bad times. But it was more good times than anything.

Being married with a new family and her job, we only saw her when she was getting off work and stopped by the house. But I noticed even though she didn't live there she would give my momma money every Friday when she got paid. She would buy us clothes. But our other older siblings bought for us as well, especially their wives. We were absolutely spoiled.

At Christmas, you couldn't have told us that we didn't move into a toy store. We never had to share our toys, because we got the same things. If we got kitchen sets for Christmas, they bought each one of us a kitchen set. We would get a camera and a tape player a piece. Victoria and I were alike. Faith would be more advanced. We just say her daddy was trying to be a big shot. But then her toys tore up quicker than ours so they must have been cheap, but then Faith was rough on toys.

Everything was going fine. We became aware that Lessie was really our mother. It didn't bother us as long as she stayed down there with her new husband. Our momma and daddy loved us to death. We were so proud that the kids knew we were not on welfare. We lived in a big house with a porch you could walk under. It was a house that some white family lived in. They built a house on the highway with an indoor bathroom. Since my daddy worked for them they let us live there. We had a fireplace in every room. We had a dining room and a living room. We had a front and back yard. Even though we lived in the country, we were happy.

Everyone was working; shoot, during the week we would hit them up for money, because a bus called the rolling store came by on Friday. He would arrive every Friday afternoon around 3:30 pm. We would stand by the mailbox, which for us was under the pecan tree, because it used to get hot in the South in the 70's. Sometimes, we would wait up to two hours. My momma would holler at my baby brother, David, my sister and me saying, y'all could have walked to the store and back by the time he comes. Knowing good and well she would not let us out of her sight. See, our momma was a God fearing woman and she didn't curse. Unless she got mad. She wouldn't let us go to the neighbor's house which was a fourth of a mile away. Besides, that store was 8 miles away.

By Friday with the change we found and the money we scrounged up we would have two dollars a piece sometimes. We would divide it three ways. But we knew Victoria wouldn't do right-she wouldn't put all her money in the pot. So she always got more. We would spend a dollar on the rolling store and save a dollar for church. See this big lady would sell a bag of peanuts, soda and cake for a dollar after church.

Daddy would say that's all the income she had for those 9 children. A dollar could go a long way back then. On the rolling store you could buy a RC cola, Sunbeam honey bun, 6 penny wheel cookies, 10 pieces of 3 cent candy and 25 pieces of 1 cent bubblegum. But this day and time, you would have to choose between a honey bun and a soda. If all you had was a dollar.

I don't know who told Lessie to get a divorce. Believe me, life as we knew it would change. The man was like one of the family. He worked with my brother. It was ugly.

When a sister gets a DE-VORCE, not a divorce, it is ugly. All the good reasons she married him goes out of the window. I mean you know he is everything to us when we are in love. He is sexy and chocolate. Chocolate means he is dark skinned or black in every sense of the word. Sexy is when he is really ugly and dresses nice... If he is thick, he really is fat. He is also the best lover and that means he can do a lot of tricks in the bed because he was not blessed down low. All that changes when you are getting a DE-VORCE. He can't dress, don't bathe, breath stinks, don't never have money, he only gives you 3 minutes of sex then he's asleep. We talk about the in-laws like it is their fault. We don't care who hears us talking about him, because you know they gonna tell it the same way. Again, it's ugly.

Lessie would curse him out. When he called-she cursed him out. She looked at my sister and me and starts cursing him out. Hell anybody that was fat she cursed him out. I thought she would calm down when she had all her teeth pulled out, but that didn't stop her. But when he called just to check on her, she went to cursing and spitting blood everywhere. Ma Bellsouth probably needs an AIDS test and a bible to repent. Because she laid down some serious cursing about him back then. You would think he would have hung up but he didn't.

After that she got her life together, and she decided to move out. We were like, ok, nice having you here. She told Victoria and me we need to get our stuff together. See, Victoria was like her. We went in our playhouse behind the barn and Victoria cursed her out. But what could we do?

Our momma and daddy did not want us to move, but we had to. They were mad. She needed us to baby sit Faith. When Victoria found that out, we went back to the playhouse and Victoria cursed her and Faith out, again. We were plotting like the kid on Leave It to Beaver of all the evils things she could do to Faith.

We moved out. It wasn't too bad but as the bitterness grew, I joined every club and played sports all year so I wouldn't be home. I was not babysitting. Not to mention, I was good in sports. So she didn't bother me. We got through it.

Lessie and I always began our conversations where she would want to talk about somebody and their children-really, she wanted to talk about me or one of mine. So when I played dumb, she would go for the gold and let me have it. She said I don't know what to say about the women going with men that don't help them. You need a man that's gonna break bread. That mean gives you money. He wouldn't lay up with me married or not married and get my stuff without making a donation. He don't have to pay tithes-but he sure as hell can do love offerings every now and then. If the booty is good, he would offer assistance. Like you. I looked up as if I wasn't paying her any attention. You want everybody to think you got it going on but you don't–you are broke. I wouldn't waste my time with that pretty nigger. I bet he hasn't given you anything but some dick.

Now my children, my sister and her kids, my nephew, and some kids from the neighborhood were present in the next room. I know they heard her. I could have hit her. I had to come back with an excuse or a black folk's lie. I said you give me time and I am going to break him in, we have just started. She said have you started giving him some if so that's when you should have started.

Some how the blood rushed to the top of my head and I couldn't control my tongue. Just because you had been sneaking round with your ex-husband since he has been married, I am not you. You meet that man 2 times a year, Christmas and Fourth of July. This is the time his job gives him bonuses. You put on that fake Versace red sundress and that Secret Deodorant and call it White Diamonds and go out for an hour and a half. Don't make you an expert. That is not me. She said you weren't mad when I gave you some of the money. I just turned and walked out of the door.

I went to one person that I know when I see her it would be alright.

My momma. When I explained to her what happened, she said you know she just jealous. You got to live and make your own mistakes.

## Chapter 21

Conflict, Drama and Controversy must have been my First, Middle and Last name. They stayed in my life. I did not know how much I could take. My grandmother would get upset with me about the least little thing. Her patience was wearing thin. Constantly reminding me of what someone would say about us living with her. She would say they say you don't have anywhere to go or how long will it be before you move. I knew when I disrespected my mother I drew first blood in her eyes and the Lord's eyes.

Just my luck, the deal for the first house fell through. The contractor undermined the agent. The seller backed out. But how can you explain that to an elderly woman. So, I had to find a new house to buy. One day when I came home from work I was depressed and stressed and we got into a heated augment. My grandmother and I just blew up. I didn't disrespect her, though. But, with nowhere to go I loaded up the children and all the clothes I could get and left. I called my uncle who lived in a nearby town who rented out houses. I needed to know if he had any vacancies available. He did not want me to rent the house because of the neighborhood and I couldn't live with him. He suggested that I make up with my grandmother. I was stubborn. I was not hearing that shit. Michael said I could move into a house in Macon that his godmother owned. He knew that was not an option especially since I can barely afford to drive to my job which is 25 miles away. How could I afford to drive to Macon which is 75 miles away? I'm saving all my money to move. Lessie wanted me to get a trailer like my sister, but I wasn't satisfied with a trailer.

I chose an option that I knew was unspeakable. I knew the kids wouldn't like it. I chose to live with Howard. I called him and he said come on. I said thank you. He put me in this predicament anyway he needed to help out. If he would have acted right, I wouldn't be homeless. So we moved in with him. Howard and I kept in contact through Cameron, even though Michael and I were seeing each other. He hated Michael and Michael hated him. When times were tight Howard would help me out. I paid him back every penny. I didn't want Michael in my business just yet. I hid my financial situation from him.

I lied to Michael and told him I was staying with my uncle. I told him since he was married he couldn't come around and my uncle knew he was married. So that meant he couldn't call me or stop by. Michael bought it I guess. He never questioned me. I didn't even tell my family where we were. Because I am sure someone would find out and tell it. So I said let them find out the best way they can.

When we arrived I went over the ground rules with the kids. I told them do not call and let anyone know where we are. I need a couple days of rest. I told them if they call someone to block the number. I made arrangements to help Howard with the bills. I told him no sex under any condition. He agreed not to tell anyone since he worked with Michael. The apartment was a 2 bedroom. The children used a blow up mattress in their room to sleep on. I slept on that pretend-to-be leather sofa. The children said they would sleep with their door open because they didn't trust Howard. I complained that I had a hard day at work. Moving here had me driving an hour and 10 minutes to work one way. I usually drove 30 minutes to work one way before. So I told him I needed to take a shower and turn in to bed early. He understood.

All I wanted to do was take a shower and go to sleep. He cooked dinner for the kids. The kids were happy because they had cable TV. My grandmother had 4 channels. She was still living in the 70s when it came to her TV. She still had one of those big tall antennas that looked like an airplane was on top of it. I slept so peacefully that night even though I almost sweated to death. No worries. I did not worry about what my family thought of me. Since someone kept insisting that I was taking advantage of my mother by living there with her.

## Chapter 22

I knew I couldn't afford it. Come With US Entertainment was planning another trip to Myrtle Beach, South Carolina. I had all my money tied up with the house. I had to get out of Howard's house. He was trying to get attached. I lied and said I was going with Michael anyway-this was to let Howard know I was serious about Michael. Here I was living with Howard and planning to go out of town with another man. Now Howard seemed fine with it because he knew I was dating Michael but somehow it didn't seem right. I didn't hide that I was going out of town with Michael.

I was open and honest with Howard. I tried not to give him any false hope while staying there. I was keeping my distance.

But whenever we engaged in conversation he would convincingly say it is him that I love. He just messed up and I need to learn to forgive him. I would say you know when I quit someone I never go back no matter what. That is my golden rule.

The house wasn't gonna be ready until September 15. The family needed a month to move out. They had been trying to sell it for a year. You would think they would have that shit ready to go. I wanted to be out of Howard's house before the South Carolina trip. If I have some money left from settling the house deal I was going. It looked like it wasn't gonna happen. But I waited patiently.

Off and on Howard would remind me that maybe the Lord sent the children and me back to him. I would say it was not the Lord; the Lord would have told you to marry us in the first place; and we would not be in this mess. I would tell him I don't love you any more. You are a good friend to me now and that is all you will ever be. He said you will see.

So to keep down confusion, I would not talk to Michael in his house on the phone. I would leave for work earlier so I could meet Michael.

I would go to a payphone and call him if I wanted to talk. Meanwhile Michael still didn't know I was residing with Howard. At least he said he didn't. Howard didn't want anybody to know either. Especially since he had dogged me out to his close coworkers. Making it seem like the breakup was my fault. So, how could he take me back? I knew he was lying, about wanting me back. It was his way of showing me you are not gonna have anyone in your life.

I began to debate about going to South Carolina because the kids and my financial situation were not the greatest. The children wanted me to go again. They still were angry with Howard. He knew it too. No matter what he did for them while we were there, they kept their guard up. But not Cameron-he was like a little puppy-he looked up to him. Cameron loved him.

The week of the trip I was making my last minute efforts to go. I was still trying to find a bona fide excuse not to go instead of just saying no, I can't afford it. Now I really was trying to live like the Jones. Besides that, Michael knew he didn't have any extra money either. He has borrowed money from me on occasion even though he has paid me back. I didn't have time or money to help someone out if they lose their money again.

Just as I made up my mind not to go on the trip, Howard got sick. A nurse called me and said he had to have emergency surgery and will be placed in ICU. I had noticed Howard's health was failing. He also was losing weight. I said, perfect. When I called Michael I lied on Cameron and said he was so distraught and upset over Howard that I could not leave him. Especially, if he died I would feel so guilty knowing I wasn't there for my son. Michael acted as if he bought it. He knew how Cameron felt about Howard. He knew what he went through when Howard and I broke up, because I told him.

When we walked in ICU at Mayview Park Hospital all his family was there. They looked at me like where was I going. Now Howard had said his folks didn't have any problem with me. He said they still liked me especially his grandmother. The woman looked at me and turned her head like she had seen a monster. I pretended I didn't see that and spoke to everyone. The kids and I proceeded to go in and see Howard. His mother and Aunt Mae who were sitting in the waiting room got up and followed us.

They stood in the corner while we visited. He smiled so weakly like he was about to die. I'm glad you didn't go to South Carolina. You don't need to waste your life with a married man he says. His family started whispering. I said to myself, just lay there and tell them all my business.

But what pissed me off more about his family was how nasty they were treating the children and me. I wished I had gone to South Carolina. I thought he's just a big liar like me. I pretended to be polite and courteous and got the hell out of there.

After our visit the children and I went to get something to eat. When we returned to the house the door was locked. The whole while we were staying there the door was never locked. He had been in the hospital for 2 days and now the door was locked. I began to wonder did I lock the door by mistake. He didn't lock it, because he only had one key. We know it was not safe, but because of our work hours someone was at the apartment the majority of the time. The apartment was empty on an average of only 2-3 hours a day.

Since I did not have my cell phone with me, and it was after visiting hours, I drove to a pay phone and called Howard at the hospital. He said his mom must have locked it, because she went by to pick up some items. I asked him if you needed something why didn't you ask me to bring it. He had no answer. I asked him for her number. He said it was private. I asked him to call her so I can get the key, because I knew she didn't like me. This would cut down confusion. He said he would. I told him I would go over to her house.

When I pulled up I could see her through the screen door. It was an old house. From the looks of the outside it needed to be condemned. But the inside as I remember it was nice. So never judge a book by its cover. When I got out of the car she had made it out onto the porch. I said hey, how are you doing? She said fine thanks for asking. I asked her had Howard called her. She said no. I'm thinking this old hag is going to make me beg. So I told her he was supposed to call you so you can give me the key to his apartment. She said why. I thought to myself none of your damn business, but I explained our living situation and I added that we would be out by the end of next week-our house will be ready.

So she turned as if she were going to get the key. But I heard her on the telephone. Whoever she was talking to she gave them hell-it was probably Howard. When she returned she said in a nasty tone you need to bring the key back. I said no problem. I told her I'll bring it right back. Then she said no you can wait until the morning. Her attitude changed, I guessed she realized that she didn't need to be mad at me. She needs to deal with her son. So I agreed to bring the key back in the morning before I go to work. She began to be more pleasant. She asked me again how long I had been staying with Howard. I told her about two months now. She just nodded her head. Meanwhile I told myself I had to make an appointment with Howard to air some things out.

I knew I had to get out of his house.

## Chapter 23

I visited Howard several times at the hospital. His health appeared to be improving. But it didn't matter when I visited with Howard at the hospital, his Aunt Mae or mom was present. Like, they were guarding him. I'm thinking I don't want him I am being concerned. So I called him mostly. This one time I showed up early so I could beat them there. The hospital intensive care unit rules were for visitation to begin at 10:00 am. So I figured I could go early and see him. Guess what? His aunt was there, again. Instead of him asking her for privacy, he would let them stay and listen to our conversation. I wanted to talk to him about what was wrong with him. Why was he sick?

Since, I didn't have a choice but to have a discussion with her present, I told him that the house would be ready next week. The kids and I would be moving. He said he didn't think he would be out of the hospital for a couple of weeks. I was fine with that. Shit, I was elated. I would be out of his apartment before he came home. This was Tuesday when we talked.

Friday, I came home from work. I walked into the apartment with my head down. I finally looked up. He was sitting there. I could not believe my eyes. He said that he was taking up space and that home health care could come by and see about him. I said really. I was shocked; I knew he was not well. Who could get themselves released from Intensive Care Unit within a week? I asked him how was he doing. He said fine. He asked me about work. I answered the same old drama as usually and I am glad I got a job.

I am thinking again, what, he must have thought we were going to steal from him. I looked around. Hell, he ain't got nothing worth taking. Because it was late, I told him I was turning in early.

Before I made myself comfortable, after my shower, I asked him if I needed to get him anything to eat. He said, yes, you. I laughed and said you are not well for those kinds of activities. I knew he was serious. He said you been here for two months, you know I want you. I said I appreciate what you have done for me. But I do not feel that way. He said you do not have to feel that way for us to do this.

I really was not trying to get in a standoff since I hadn't moved yet. I noticed he had that look in his eye. I said it is that time of month. He said well you haven't moved yet. You owe me one night with you. I was saved by mother nature even though it was a lie. How many times have I used that lie in the past? Headaches don't work for black women.

Next evening when I came in, he asked how everything was going. I said good. I told him the kids were spending the weekend at my mom's house. They would not be in his way this weekend. I told him that I had to work this weekend and would probably be getting home late. I told him he could get plenty of rest and quiet in the apartment. I grabbed a soda and went into the room where the kids slept. I tried everything to go to sleep. I am so used to lying on the sofa and falling asleep with the TV on. So, I had to wait until he went to his room and go to sleep before I came out.

The last day before the move, I was lightly sleeping and I felt someone rubbing my face. It was Howard. He had gotten into the bed beside me. He slowly moved his hand under my t-shirt and attempted to get me aroused. He whispered I know it is off because I have been checking the sanitary supply in the bathroom. He began to rub my breast harder and kissed me. He knew what excited me from our past relationship, by doing oral sex. He lowered his self between my legs and started to lick me slowly all over my vagina. I tried not to like it, but I couldn't help it. When he finished, he climbed on top of me and penetrated me. I thought, now I know how a prostitute feels. He worked up a sweat. I pretended it was good by moaning and breathing heavy. I tried to pretend it was ok. I felt so sick. He asked me did it feel good. I said yes, I am ready to cum. He then climaxed and whispered to me I love you. But I always knew when he let us stay here that he wanted more. He wouldn't even take the money to help him out with the bills. Luckily, it didn't take long and he was through. He wanted to cuddle and talk. All I wanted to do was get up and take a shower. After a few minutes, I asked if he wanted some breakfast. I would have used any excuse to get out of bed with him. It worked.

I cooked breakfast. While we were eating, I said please do not interpret what happened last night in the wrong way. He said no, I won't. He said it was for old time's sake. He asked did you enjoy it. I got up from the table and walked to the counter. I had my back to him and I said it was ok. I was rolling my eyes in the back of my head. He just didn't know I would have done anything for my children. He used this situation to get what he wanted. I used him for a place to stay for my family.

# Chapter 24

We were finally settled in our new home. The kids were happy. It was in the city limits. It was a three bedroom home with all the works. It was not handicapped accessible for Howard, so, he could not visit. I knew he would want to. All I could focus on was repairing my relationship with Michael. He helped us move the stuff out of storage. We were connecting, again.

I knew Howard still had feelings for me, I did not know how deep. When he got back to work, somehow it got out. The street committee knew that I did not go to South Carolina with Welch. I supposedly stayed here to take care of Howard. I wonder who told the street committee. Let me guess. Howard, Howard, or Howard. Michael became more and more distant. Cameron became an ally for Howard. He would say Howard was good to us-he gave us a place to stay. He asked don't you want to work it out with him? I said no-it is not that simple.

Michael had stopped by. Cameron entered the living room and said Howard called you momma. I had to play it off. I asked what did he call for. He said mommy you and Howard talked everyday. Michael didn't say anything, but I knew he wanted to confront me.

Then times began to get bad. I was fighting to pay bills and the expenses for the children and me. We weren't eligible for any benefits. So I began by writing checks just to juggle everything. Bouncing checks was a stall delay to keep the utilities on until I got paid. I knew it would take a 7 to 10 day turnaround. The checks would bounce once. By the time they would send it through again my work check, which was direct deposit, would be in the bank.

I wanted to get a part time job. But the way my work schedule and the children's activities were it would have been difficult. Who would pick them up? Since, I had alienated my family I know I couldn't ask for help. So, I didn't see getting a part time job as an option.

I was waiting on a child support refund. They finally were able to get some of my arrears through stopping Josh, Cameron and Sean's sperm donor income tax check. It would definitely be a plus for the budget. It would put us in the black with a little to go in the bank. But it wasn't coming fast enough. The one child support check I had been getting in a timely matter, which was from Kira's dad, began to come later and later. Instead of every month, it was coming every six weeks. He knew that after six week they would give you a notification that they will be suspending his license. So then he would go make a payment.

The first two months were going to be difficult. In the beginning, the agent was only asking the first month's rent in advance. Right before we signed she said she needed a deposit also. It was to pay her fees. I was so desperate to move in. I didn't question her. I gave it to her. I didn't want to stay with Howard any longer. So my bank account went in the red.

One night I heard Cameron crying. I asked him what is wrong. He said Howard was the only father he knew and he wanted us to live with him. I said you can have him-I don't want him. I told him he was a good person but that relationship is in the past. I told him if it makes him feel better he can go visit him on the weekends and Howard can still come visit him at games. He seemed ok. I knew he was communicating with Howard too much.

I got a message from the school to call. I knew it was going to be about Cameron. He decided he was going to be Robin Hood. He started stealing and taking money. He was going into kids' lockers and gym bags. He had been caught stealing twice. This time they were talking about putting him out of school, if I didn't get counseling for him. He said the reason he was stealing was to give Sean and Kira spending money and to help me out. I wanted to call his father. But, I knew it was like getting pie thrown in my face. I knew he would say to me you can call me now they are in trouble-you never called before. I knew he wasn't gonna help, since child support took his income tax. So I put that idea out of my head. Besides, he would want a booty call. So I tried to convince Cameron there was no need to steal-the Lord will provide.

So to help out, I gave up going to get my hair done. Moria would understand since I was in a tight fix. So, I called Monica who had recently married. I could get something done which was low maintenance. I brought some hair and made up my mind to get pin plaits. Monica was going to give me a discount, which was forty dollars opposed to ninety dollars. I can keep the pin plaits approximately 3 months and save about two hundred. I loved going to get my hair done, it is the one thing I can do for myself. But, I need my electricity on, too. After Monica finished, I looked totally different. I hadn't had long hair in 12 years. And, it was good spending time with Monica. We had a chance to catch up. Since she came to my house, I gave her a tour of the home. I was so proud to show it off.

After I made Cameron apologize and return the money, he stopped stealing. He didn't get kicked out of school. But you better believe I tore that behind up and he had to wash dishes for a year. Since, you know, he had sticky hands.

# Chapter 25

Being played is sure a bitter sweet feeling. A team should always stick together-no matter what. I can't be too mad about being played. Since the beginning of time someone has been played. Remember Adam and Eve, didn't that snake play the hell out of Eve? So yes the Player Organization has been around a long time. Being played is when you lose focus. When you stopped being an individual and become a team player to someone who is not loyal to the cause. That's when you realize, you are the only one on the team. Each and every one had a hidden agenda.

The last month since the South Carolina trip that I could not go on, Michael and I hadn't been close. My phone calls weren't returned-he called less-or he just wasn't responsive to me when he came around. I know he was hurt because I did not go on the South Carolina trip, but he couldn't let me know. Too much pride, I guess. Eventually, I came to the conclusion that there was another woman. It would be my fault because I made him work at getting me all this time. The cat and mouse game I had played was almost over. It looked like I was losing.

So, I took a chance and called Bobby his best friend. Michael and Bobby became good friends after the New Orleans trip. I really admired Bobby. He was a family man. It didn't matter how many women flirted with him; he remained true to his wife. He would say this is business. Deep down I knew he didn't approve of Michael and my relationship, but he went along with it. During our conversation, Bobby talked about the trip, how nice it was and why I should have gone. I played Bobby and said why did you let Michael mess up? He said how did you know? I said he told me about her. He said he told you about what happened in the Jacuzzi? I said yes. He said he had been drinking and depressed because you did not go. I said I was shocked he slept with a total stranger. Bobby said yes that's unsafe. Bobby said you and he need to sit down and talk-really you need to work it out and get Howard out of your business-you need to decide because his wife wants a divorce-she is tired of their situation.

I said I guess it is my time to chase him, especially since he is someone else's husband. But I have never chased anyone in my life. They always chase me. I fired them when I got ready. They just kept coming back. But for the second time I thought, this was it. Remember an old saying–anything worth having is worth working for-it wouldn't just fall in your lap. But I didn't have any idea what I was up against.

This particular day, Michael called me earlier in the morning. I asked him to go out to lunch or stop by. He said he had work to do. He told me I'll call you later before I leave work. So I told him OK, I'll be home. Just so happened my plans changed and I needed to leave. So, I called him at 3:00 at work to let him know.

I talked to Kara the secretary in his department. She said where did you and Michael go to lunch? I thought about it-I said I can't tell you. Well he came back on cloud 9, not knowing she was telling on him. He said he had the best time ever. It felt good, again. I said really. I didn't say another word. I played it off.

Michael called me before he got off work and said he couldn't stop by because he had to pick up the children. I said OK. I couldn't say anything because I didn't want him to know that Kara had told on him.

For a week we did not do lunch or he didn't stop by. I asked him is something wrong-he said no. I haven't seen you, I told him. He said we have been talking. I said I know but it's not like you not to come by. I thought he must assume that I knew something. The next evening he came by but he was nervous. As if he might get caught for being here with me. We talked for a little while. He again made up an excuse so he could leave. I let him go. My pride would not let me question him. I said I needed to wait and be patient. If I have lost him, it would be for the best. BUT I DID NOT WANT TO LET GO OR I CAN'T LET GO. I was not right in the eyes of the Lord anyway.

## Chapter 26

Since the first time that I talked to Officer Catlin on the phone, I should not have trusted her. We worked together on the dorms earlier in my career. She was a drama queen. She was on the dirt committee. When you dig up dirt, you don't know what you will find. Nobody would listen to her because her dirt was usually lies and speculations. We knew each other from way back. I knew she wasn't trustworthy back then.

It wasn't a Hey how you are doing, is Counselor Welch in, no he's not, thank you, good-bye conversation. She brought up Howard and how she just knew we were getting back together or will get back together again as if she had heard that from someone reliable. She knew I would always love Howard. But everyone knew we were not getting back together. She was there at the beginning of Howard's and my relationship. She held my hand when the accident happened and prayed for me. So she knew the history, but that doesn't make her an expert on what I need now.

I became defensive, big mistake, I fell for the bait. All she had to do was take me out of the frying pan and put me on the table and serve me. I was done. I told her with no uncertainty that Howard and I were never getting back together. We were over with. I have paid my dues to the disabled community. I told her I was in love with Michael. She said I heard that Howard and you had reconciled. I said no we had not.

I guess, out of pity, she said I didn't know you felt like that. She said Michael has been seeing someone else. She asked me did I know Alisha Jefferson. I said no, I did not know her. She was trying to explain who Ms. Jefferson was and how I should know her. But at the end I still did not have a clue. I just wanted her to tell me what had been going on between Michael and her. She said I even told Jefferson that Michael and you were in a relationship. But she said that Michael and she had been seeing each other for a while. She had been driving to Macon to meet him. They had been to the mall together and held hands. He had picked out and bought some perfume for her. But I was fine until she said that Michael had taken her to our favorite restaurant and brought her White Diamonds perfume. This was the same kind he had bought for me. Then he had the nerve to invite to her to go on the next trip which was to New Orleans. I know you wandering why I didn't hang up but remember we are NO MALES.

    Here I am calling him and asking him to take me out or even just to stop by to see me! I thanked her for the information and told her that God sent me an angel, because I already knew something wasn't right. Hell all kinds of angels had been giving me words of wisdom; I wasn't listening. She was an angel-what kind I don't know yet. So everything she told me I knew was probably true. At least I felt it was true. That's what I get for going with someone's husband. How can I be mad-he doesn't belong to me.

## Chapter 27

Gossip has 4 rules: 1) 70 % of it is lies, 2) 10% is the truth or bait (the bait is just enough to make you share your thoughts and feelings), 3) 10% is like a bullet-it doesn't care who it hits (or in other words talks about). It could be anybody-Gossip doesn't discriminate, and 4) 10% What ever you say or don't say to that person they will take it back to the one you are talking about.

The numbers 2 and 4 are what got me. It was like a ritual for 10 days. Officer Catlin called me and I called her every day. She was better than the Headline News. She knew everything. I should have known that she was toting news back and forth. I clearly stated I was checking to see was he gonna called me back. He didn't call. I thought he would call me to see if I was upset. I know she told him she informed me. Because she came back and said that he had not slept with Jefferson, like I was gonna believe that. She had already told me that he was hitting it.

Michael didn't call the whole weekend. I blocked all private numbers from my house phones. So if he called me on one of them cheap cell phones, the number would show up. I was planning, if he called, to casually mention that I was having lunch with an old friend on Tuesday. I was trying to make him jealous. He called me at 10:00 am, I told him I was asleep and I would call him after lunch. Melvin, my old friend, and I had lunch at the local restaurant. There were a lot of correctional employees there having lunch. So I knew someone would tell him. I was trying to let him know yeah I can see someone else too.

Promptly at 1:30 pm he called me. Melvin was still there, so I told him I would call him back. I didn't. He called me again around 4:00 and said that was a hellified lunch date. I said he was an old friend. He said I heard. So we chit chatted for a while. He said you knew people would be looking at you and talking about your lunch date. Finally the kids came in and I said I had to go. He said we need to talk. I said when. He said now, we can talk now. I told him we need to do this in person. I arranged for us to meet on the next day. He said no let's do it now.

So I began. I explained to him that for the last two weeks I have made every effort to cut the distance between us. I felt like I was begging him to be with me. No matter what I did to communicate he gave me his ass to kiss.

So, without tipping my hand on what Officer Caitlin had told me, I acted vague in the conversation. I told him that I think for the last year I have been the best other woman ever. I had been faithful, never slept with anyone else but him-I even encouraged him to stay home with his wife and kids. I said do you think that the next woman will put up with your situation? I even mentioned to him that he wanted everyone to think that he was not married and come out in public and had announced we were lovers. I told you to keep us a secret. You were the one talking about love and marriage.

Finally, I went there, I mentioned I felt like he was seeing someone else. He admitted that he had lunch with a coworker up town but that was it. I said get real, if you had lunch-you did the rest. I said I had been a fool hoping and praying that we can really make this work the right way and you did me like this, with that I hung up.

Catlin called me 3 days later on a fishing expedition. So naturally she knew she fucked up by telling me all his business. She talked about how hurt he was. He didn't want us to end. That he wasn't seeing Officer Jefferson, they were just friends. She said that Officer Jefferson didn't want him either. She said Jefferson said he couldn't sleep with his wife and her too.

She said didn't I tell you she was married too? I said hell no that is ugly. She said Jefferson said she needs a paymaster and Michael was not it. I told her because he ain't got any money, that's why. I guess she thought this would make me feel good. I asked her why are you changing your story now. That's what happened she said. I told her I did not believe her. I told her I was tired and didn't feel like discussing the situation.

Next time she called me she said that Michael said that I needed to break all ties with Howard. I said what? You know Howard and you are too close. I told her the only reason that Howard and I were close was my son. There is no relationship. Michael often made statements about Howard but he always understood. She pissed me off. I knew then I needed to end this between her and me. She was two-faced and a liar. Everyone always says she kept up drama. But see, again I was being nosey. I said to her knowing she was going to repeat it, he is still sleeping with his wife, how can he make me decide. She said you are right. I hung up again.

Next time she called she said let me be honest. She told me he was sleeping with Ms. Jefferson and that he was trying to make it work with his wife and kids also. I said to myself that was odd because Bobby said his wife was leaving him. I thought she is confusing me more and more. I asked her to quit torturing me. I'm through. He is a grown ass man and he needs to talk to me. I told her there was no need for her call me back and I won't be calling her back-I don't care what happens-I got to go out of town, and I don't need to hear from you or him.

# Chapter 28

Deception-Confiding in Howard was very bad- He knew all my short comings and down falls-things that I could never tell Michael. So when things were not good, I confided in him. Even though we had a bad break up, we stayed friends for my son Cameron's sake. He would come to all of his games. He wanted him there. Even when Michael and I would be there he would show up like a proud father. I guess I was too embarrassed to tell my girlfriends or Michael the things I was going through. I wanted Michael to think I was perfect.

I ended all contact with Officer Catlin due to drama. I was trying to live at peace. Howard felt the need to start calling more and more. He fed me rumor after rumor about Michael. I sat there and ate it up. Tuesday, Howard mentioned how two of his coworkers Lisa and Tammy struck up a conversation about Welch. He told me how he was chasing secretaries and female officers. He said Lisa stated Michael was flirting with her and she felt uncomfortable. Everyone knew Howard and Michael didn't get along, and I couldn't help but wonder why they would do such a thing. Both Lisa and Tammy were very close to Michael. After almost a week of debating, I began to start believing Howard. What could he gain by lying-he knew it was over between him and me. All I had been doing is confessing to him on how much I really loved Michael. It was Michael that I really wanted to be with. Howard seems to really understand my decision.

So, I called Lisa. She told me no-she wouldn't dare do that, the same with Tammy. All I could think was why would Howard lie? You told me you didn't want me. So when I confronted him, he acted so innocent. He said who you gonna believe. They like him and they're just trying to make me look bad. So I guess I fell for it. Since Michael was acting so funny, I just left well enough alone. I didn't want any tension on their job. God knows there was enough of it.

Tuesday, Michael called me and said he was gonna call me back. He didn't call. So I said I'll call him when he gets to work. Well I called his dorm. He was either busy or away from his desk. I left a message with Lisa. So about 4:00 pm, I called Lisa and she said she gave him the message. She said he acted all surprised to have heard from me as if I wasn't supposed to call him.

So between 5:00 pm and 6:00 pm, I called where he usually is working. I didn't get an answer. So I finally called the control room operator, she couldn't hold water: she told me that he did not want any calls from anyone and if anyone asked she didn't know where he was. I said, really. But see I'm stubborn, I wanted to know where he was, what had I done to him, why is he avoiding me and why is he angry with me. We always said we will be friends to the end. This is how you treat a friend?

So after careful consideration I decided to wait for him when he got off work. Because we agreed that something is bothering us we would always talk about it. I didn't hold up my end of the deal but he didn't know that or did he?

I promise you I got this bad feeling that finally our relationship was over. No matter if it was I didn't want it to be over. I sat on the sofa and cried. I asked God to help me through this. I know he wouldn't because Michael was still married. I saw all the writing on the wall. I saw the signs in the sky. I didn't want to read them. Yes, I was in denial. But I had to know. I don't know why especially since I had been trying to end it for six months. Now that I am caught up in the relationship, he is trying to let me loose.

I was waiting in the parking lot. I did not park near his vehicle, because I did not want him to go back inside when he saw me. As he approached his truck, I stepped outside my car. I called his name. He turned and looked at me. He was totally shocked to see me standing there. I asked him what is going on, what is the problem. If there is something you need to tell me, just tell me. I said you got me looking like a fool. You won't return my calls. I just want to know if it is over. I want you to tell me to my face, so I can go on with my life. We are supposed to be friends. Friends don't treat each other like this. I asked why I am getting all this bad information. He said you need to stop talking to them that is the problem. I said you won't talk to me. Even though I didn't really want to hear what he had to say, because I already knew in my heart that it was over.

Finally, he said I just don't want to see you anymore. Howard will not go away. I don't think you want him to go away either. So it's best that we call it off.

At first I was just angry but I knew better than to let someone see you at your lowest. My mother instilled that in me in my raising. I retreated as if to give up. I swallowed and said thank you, you be good and I won't call you anymore. He stepped up to me and hugged me. I couldn't hug him back, because I would just crumble if I did. He walked away. I walked back to my car and got in. I drove off first to let him know that I was going along with his wishes.

Once I made it home, I put the kids to bed. I was staring at the ceiling and letting the tears roll. Father time had won. The plan did not work. Deep down inside, my plan was to get in the new house and get everything situated, so when Michael left home he would come be with me. So, all the lying and being secretive was a waste of time. It did not work.

The phone rang. It was Howard. It was like he could read my mind when I'm in trouble. I told him everything. He said I know how you feel. He said go to sleep and I'll check on you tomorrow.

## Chapter 29

Thursday I cried so much you would have thought someone died. I waited until the kids got on the bus. I couldn't let them know how I was so hurt and disappointed. They have suffered enough. I really wasn't crying over losing over a lover, but I lost my best friend. Someone I had become attached to.

Howard called me that morning on his way to work. He said he was gonna stop by and see me before he went to work just to check on me. I had told him what happened. When he stopped by, I came outside. I was walking slowly toward him. Before I could make it to his car, I burst into tears. I couldn't stop crying. He held me and said it was gonna be alright. If it's meant to be it'll happen. He said he didn't deserve me anyway.

After I pulled myself together, he opened the car door and pulled me in so I could sit in his lap. He lifted my head up and gave me two kisses on the lips. But the third one he tried to French kiss me-he tried to put his tongue in my mouth. I pulled back. I told him don't do that. I mean it felt so nasty. I could have thrown up. Here I am grieving and he was gonna try to make a move on me. I became angry. He tried to apologize. He said he didn't mean anything by it. I said yeah right.

I made an excuse that I had to make a phone call and I'll call him later. As I walked back to the house, I looked back at him-he had this kind of smirk on his face. I said I'll question him later about that. Now I just want to go to my sanctuary (my sofa).

After he left, I assumed the position on the sofa. I was lying there in the dark, watching a Lifetime movie. Then Howard called me from work. He made me promise not to say anything to anybody. My whole body froze, I almost freaked out. What have I done now I thought to myself? He went on to tell me that Michael went to Barbara (the Superintendent's Assistant) and told her that I had been calling him. He also told her that I confronted him in the parking lot as if I were stalking him. My eyes were bigger that two light bulbs at this time. He said that Barbara told the Superintendent. The Superintendent and the Chief of Security were talking about me and my behavior. He said the Chief of Security told him about it. He said you know me and the Chief of Security are good friends. He was telling me to check on you. I said Holy Shit. I would have never thought that Michael hated me that much to tell them that I was stalking him. I could get fired. We are never to mix personal lives with our job. Fraternization is a definite no. So I promised Howard again I would not say anything.

# Chapter 30

I sat there for awhile in a daze. Thinking what have I got myself into? But I can hear Lessie say do what you do best: prove and defend. She loved to tell me that. She would say that's why nobody will not tell you anything. I would say they can tell me as long as it is not a lie. I hate when people talk about what they don't know.

I called Barbara because we used to work together, too. We were close and she was actually like another mother in my life. When I worked there as a secretary she was the lead secretary so she took on the mother role. She sort of looked after me when I worked there. When I asked her did Welch report anything about me, she sounded as she didn't have a clue what I was talking about. She told me someone's been lying to you. You need to talk to the Superintendent.

At this time she put the Superintendent on the phone. Again I explained who I was and explained the situation. He didn't know what I was talking about. The only thing he could say was you need to keep your personal business away from the job and don't listen to hearsay. I informed him that I appreciated the words of advice and that I would be informing my Superintendent and there would be no more problems. Then he asked who told you this. I said Darius Howard. He said OK. I didn't care about Howard getting into trouble as long as I did not lose my job.

A few minutes later, Howard called me. He sounded as if he were crying. He was upset. Didn't I tell you not to say anything to anybody? I said yeah, but the way you were talking that man could have called my Superintendent on me. I said you know what I did. I said I went and approached that man on his job I could have gotten fired for it. I just want them to know my side. He said that's not the point-I trusted you with confidential information and you betrayed me. He said The Superintendent called Michael and me in his office along with the Chief of Security and cursed us both out. How do you think I feel getting cursed out in front of him? I said how you think I felt not knowing they may have called my job. He said you gonna jeopardize my job. I said no I was trying to save my job, thank you.

So I changed the subject, I said both Barbara and the Superintendent said they didn't know what I was talking about. So, why did you lie? He said I did not lie-the Superintendent didn't want you to know he said it. At this time he hung up. I said I know he didn't hang up on me-he is the one that is wrong.

I quickly called my job and talked to my Superintendent. I explained to her every detail. She said girl, this is better than a soap opera. She said you need to wait awhile and go after Mr. Welch. She said let everything die down. It sounds like to me Mr. Howard has issues. You need to cut off all contact, if you want Mr. Welch. I said I know. She said your child needs to understand that Howard is not who you want. Before we hung up, she said keep me informed and went to laughing. She said child he messed you up. I hung up.

I didn't let her know that I used Howard and he was angry and this is his way of getting back at me. He got me good too. But my Superintendent was a woman-she could read between the lines.

## Chapter 31

Everyone has someone that you can confess to. Be it a big sister, brother or a childhood friend or maybe your parents. I had my hairstylist. She was like a priest. She had been through as much as I had. She was a Christian sister.

Her chair was like going to confession. She was my priest. You can't see her face. She would stand behind you doing your hair. As you confessed, she listened attentively. When she responds, she doesn't judge you. She judged the act or the behavior. She does not sugar coat it. A lot of people don't appreciate it when someone is straightforward. But I do. She's gonna tell you what you need to do by the bible whether you like it or not. She's so spiritual. It is unbelievable.

So when I am through confessing, she said I know you want him to leave his wife but he won't. But for some reason I believe he loved you. He was just trying to make sure you were worth it. But you allowed him to have his cake and eat it too. I said I'm not cake, I'm ice cream and I'll melt away. She said you need to melt away. She said when push come to shove his wife knows he cheats and doesn't care. That's why he's not gonna leave. She also said if he leaves her for you, he will leave you the same way. The same way you got him is the same way you would lose him. She said you are not in Disneyland where everything is happily ever after. Those words brought a bitter taste to my mouth. I already knew it. She reminded me you live in Williamsville.

Wake up. As she turned me around, I looked in the mirror. My hair was together. I smiled and said thank you. I said thank you for my hair and those words. I looked gorgeous. I told her I'll see in church on Sunday. She said good. But I knew I wasn't going to church-I didn't feel like I deserved to be in the Lord's presence. I was ashamed.

As I squirmed in my seat she turned me around and said I love you-you are my friend. She said you can do better-wait on the Lord; he will bless you with a companion. As I drove home I said she was right. It was those hormones that won't let you wait.

# Chapter 32

I made up in my mind it was over-I started living like an inmate in lockdown. I was trying to get Michael Welch out of my system. In lockdown you only come out one time a day for recreation-one hour. In fear of running into Michael I just scheduled anything that I had to do in the daytime during the hours he was at work. I didn't want him to think I was running him down. Yes, secretly I wished that he would stop by and surprise me, but I knew that would not happen. So, I hid out. My friend Mary thought I was crazy. She said you don't have to do that.

So for a month and 10 days no contact, I went to work and home. I was trying desperately to get over my addiction. I had the urges and the need to see and talk to him, to see that gorgeous smile that he had.

One night I was riding to work-something kept telling me that I was going to see him. I just had that feeling. There he was parked beside the road. It looked as if he was having car trouble. I kept riding. I thought this fucker is no good let his ass walk to Macon or call one of those whores-I am not stopping. But the good that was in me would not let me be nasty. So I turned around. He knew what time I go to work, this is his way to test me, and I know it is. But I was weak and I did want to see him. When I approached him he said he was on the cell phone with a friend. He had a bad signal and pulled over. I said ok. He asked how I was doing and how were the kids. He said he missed me. I said I was late to work. He said you are always late to work. I smiled and drove off. I was happy. I got my fix for the month.

I tried not to fantasize or read too much into the meeting. But I could not help myself. I daydreamed what would have happened if he got out of his truck and opened my door and pulled me out of my car and began kissing me. We would have had hot and heated sex beside the road just like old times. He would have loved me until all the pain went away. I could hear him tell me we both made a mistake-he truly loved me and we would be together forever. But a deer was standing beside the road where I had the accident as if to remind me you need to leave that man alone. When I got to work I pulled out my bible and read a scripture.

Next Wednesday I went to work late intentionally, so I wouldn't run into him. I had gotten down to talking to Mary, Evelyn, and Barbara once a week, his coworkers who said they were looking out for me. I believed they were. They all said they had been through this before, being dumped. I was doing good. I noticed they never called me. I guess they were tired of talking about the same things-it was getting old. I always called them. As Bobby said too many people in your business. I kept reminding them do not let anyone know. But when I did talk to them it was my secret way of keeping up with him.

# Chapter 33

I took some time off from work. I needed every one of the seven days of doing nothing. In the beginning the Lord created the earth in 7 days. It was beautiful. I will be beautiful at the end. I just wanted to rest, sleep and watch TV. I know you're saying that's not working on yourself. Yes it is, in my book. I wanted to live like a monk. Since living like an inmate didn't work. So, I figured I'll try being a monk.

Off and on during this ordeal, Mary, whose shoulders I cried on more than Evelyn and Barbara, gave me a scripture to read. Like I said she had been through the MMS disease too. The married men syndrome. Every morning I decided to start my day when I got out of bed with this scripture Psalms 25.

## PSALMS 25

1     *Unto thee, O LORD, do I lift up my soul.*
2     *O my God, I trust in thee:*
       *let me not be ashamed,*
       *let not mine enemies triumph over me.*
3     *Yea, let none that wait on thee be ashamed:*
       *let them be ashamed which transgress without cause.*
4     *Show me thy ways, O LORD;*
       *teach me thy paths.*
5     *Lead me in thy truth, and teach me:*
       *for thou art the God of my salvation;*
       *on thee do I wait all the day.*
6     *Remember, O LORD, thy tender mercies and thy loving-kin nesses; for they have been ever of old.*
7     *Remember not the sins of my youth, nor my transgressions:*
       *according to thy mercy remember thou me*
       *for thy goodness' sake, O LORD.*

| | |
|---|---|
| 8 | *Good and upright is the LORD:* |
| | *therefore will he teach sinners in the way.* |
| 9 | *The meek will he guide in judgment:* |
| | *and the meek will he teach his way.* |
| 10 | *All the paths of the LORD are mercy and truth* |
| | *unto such as keep his covenant and his testimonies.* |
| 11 | *For thy name's sake, O LORD,* |
| | *pardon mine iniquity; for it is great.* |
| 12 | *What man is he that feareth the LORD?* |
| | *Him shall he teach in the way that he shall choose.* |
| 13 | *His soul shall dwell at ease;* |
| | *and his seed shall inherit the earth.* |
| 14 | *The secret of the LORD is with them that fear him;* |
| | *and he will show them his covenant.* |
| 15 | *Mine eyes are ever toward the LORD;* |
| | *for he shall pluck my feet out of the net.* |
| 16 | *Turn thee unto me, and have mercy upon me;* |
| | *for I am desolate and afflicted.* |
| 17 | *The troubles of my heart are enlarged:* |
| | *O bring thou me out of my distresses.* |
| 18 | *Look upon mine affliction and my pain;* |
| | *and forgive all my sins.* |
| 19 | *Consider mine enemies; for they are many;* |
| | *and they hate me with cruel hatred.* |
| 20 | *O keep my soul, and deliver me:* |
| | *let me not be ashamed; for I put my trust in thee.* |
| 21 | *Let integrity and uprightness preserve me;* |
| | *for I wait on thee.* |
| 22 | *Redeem Israel, O God,* |
| | *out of all his troubles.* |

I gave you all 22 verses for a reason you will see in the end. But right now verses 16 through 21 are what I am going through. So let me breakdown these verses in layman terms.

So this was my prayer: Yes I needed mercy. I was desolate and afflicted. My heart was enlarged with troubles. I asked the Lord to bring me out of these distresses. I know the Lord will see my affliction and pain. I believed he would forgive me of all my sins. I hoped anyway. That is if and when I stopped doing them. I only have one enemy-myself. I can't blame anyone else, even though I want to. Lord if you deliver me I will put my trust in thee and wait on thee with integrity and uprightness. Lord, relieve me from Michael and take me out of my troubles. Amen.

# Chapter 34

Day One

The first morning I was watching Oprah-I looked at her. I said she makes me sick. This particular day she was doing her Oprah favorite things show. This is where she passed out merchandise to the audience. Most of the time they are majority white. You can tell that the camera tries to focus on the black audience members to appeal to us. I thought why don't you bring that show and your stuff to the country where lower working class can get a piece of the action. Not everyone can afford an airline ticket, hotel expenses and a ticket to your show to see what size she is this week. We want a piece of the action. We can barely afford to watch her ass on cable television. That's when I knew I was bitter with myself. This woman has given millions and I'm mad at her. I dozed off back to sleep. I said McKenzie stop tripping.

Day 2

On the second day, I saw a movie on Lifetime. A woman found out that her husband had been cheating on her. She found out that the woman is someone that worked with her husband and began stalking her. I was sitting on the sofa encouraging her to find her and beat her ass. I said don't kill her just let her know she needs to leave your man alone. Then I realized that could have been me getting stalked. I am encouraging her to beat my ass.

I turn to another channel and watch The Price is Right. Something that was safe.

Day 3

I decided to watch the soap operas today-no more Lifetime movies. Don't get me wrong, they are good, but yesterday hit home. I'll watch the ones that don't apply to me. Besides that I am taking out the plaits.

They have served their purpose, TV guide.

I hate the stories-It takes a year before they get to the end of the plot. Brook done slept with the Forester's family tree on the Bold and Beautiful. Victor on the Young and the Restless done married everybody but Ms. Chancellor. But I got to give them both credit-they must have some good stuff. Everybody that done hit it keeps coming back. They never leave anyone as an enemy. But then I wandered about why they never go to church unless it is a wedding or someone is in the hospital. You know, they are hooked up to the life support machine and the next few hours are critical. They wear that little chapel out. It looked like the same chapel on every soap opera. You know they are not going to die unless you read they got a new contract on a new show. They wear that little chapel out putting on. But everybody loved them.

It's funny when they die and show up on another show in a couple days. They're still crying and getting over them being dead on the last show. It's even funnier when they can't find the body; you know they'll be back from the dead sometime. But we all get hooked on soap opera.

Then we try to imitate them, you know like having sex wearing makeup and a new hairdo. Spending all that money knowing you gonna sweat it out. Sometimes he doesn't even notice. Dummy, they have makeup artists and hairstylists standing five feet from their bed. If anybody is standing near our bed we have got caught, cheating. Anyway you know you gonna sweat that hair out if you are having good sex. If you are not, you need to let him know unless he paid for the hair. Why did I mention hair, I need to finish taking these pin plaits out of my hair that I started on Day 2.

## Day 4

I said no TV. I planned on reading a book. So I went to my personal library. It is so elaborate. It is a cardboard box that I got from behind a store when I was moving. My library is in the bottom of my closet. I had a nice collection. There was Zane with her freaky self-she taught me plenty of tricks, good looking Eric Jerome Dickey-I bought his first book because he looks good but I read the book-he can write better than he looks, and my John Grisham court room novels-since I work for the prison it was educational, just to name a few. Oooh don't let me forget Terry McMillian-she taught all the sistahs how to get their groove back, we just can't fly to Jamaica to do it.

But since I was mad at the brother I chose this book On Down Low. I had it for a year but I was scared to read it. He may have been talking about one of my ex boyfriends. Especially, the one that I went with that sang in the choir. You will read about him in Book Number 3.

Day 5

Friday-Where has the week gone? I started sleeping during the day and up all night, reading books. It hit me nobody had called me to check on me. I guess they say she is old news. I got up and looked in the mirror. I looked a mess. I called Moria. I said you need to make me beautiful. It's been rough. She said come on. When you've been with your stylist for over 10 years you got it like that. They worked you in because you are a regular. Yes she did need an update on me. I was ready to give her one because I know she don't repeat my business.

Day 6

I went home-I went to look at the monument that loved me from day one. My grandmother. I needed to be in the presence of her beauty, grace and class. She is now 79. She was a temple not looking a day over 50. The only cosmetic she uses to alter her appearance is Ms. Clairol Flame 33 with peroxide. This is what she used to dye her hair. That is some good stuff. She had been using it for 40 years. God has been good to her. I hope he will do the same for me.

She lit up when she saw me. I could feel her energy and her power embrace me. She asked when are you coming to church. I said I don't know. I said you know I work all the time. She said yes you do, but you won't be working when they have your funeral at church will you. I laughed. She was right. During our visit she gave me my favorite soda Pepsi and she gave me the update on all the family members. She said you know you are welcome here anytime you want. We talked for a little while longer. A game was coming on TV. I knew she was through talking. Like me she loves all sports. So before I left I gave her a hug and kiss. I felt revived.

I was going home to do some early spring cleaning. I will put some Jazz on and cook for the children. While I was cooking they said she's back. I said yes I am.

Day 7

I woke up Sunday morning. I had a terrible dream. I dreamt there were a lot of green and black snakes crawling everywhere. They were not biting me they were just crawling. There was one beautiful light brown one with black markings on his back just staring at me. He looked like a cobra. He was just smiling. Just as he moved toward me I woke up. I checked my sofa looking for a snake. I looked under it. I even moved the pillow. There was nothing there.

I turned on the TV and began flipping through the channels. I saw this beautiful black woman. She was dressed so elegantly. She was giving her testimony. She talked about how she went from rags to riches-riches to rags. She talked about her addictions and past relationships. The audience was crying and so was I. You think you been through it all until you've heard someone else's story. She said she found peace in his home. The home was of her Lord, Jesus Christ and the Holy Ghost, then she sang this song called Peace. I kept wandering who is she-isn't she ashamed of all that she said she has done? I wouldn't have told anyone. But here she is on national TV telling her business. I wasn't judging her but that took courage. When she finished she said she was from Waycross Georgia. I said I don't know anybody from Georgia would do that. Her name was Juanita Bynum.

I always hated to go to the Lord when I was down, broke, or going through something. You don't need him when you're up-Oh why come running when you are down? But this time was different. None of the above reasons applied. I just needed him to give me peace. I needed the word. I was ashamed of my act. To be real with you, he was there the whole time losing the house, Michael losing the money, bad supervisors, car accident, Kira's accident, Cameron's accident, and Howard's dirt. He was letting me know, I took you through it so you can come back to me. He is what I need.

I picked up my pillow and blanket like the little boy in Charlie Brown and got in my bed. I went into a peaceful sleep. I awoke around 9:30. I got up. I got the children up and announced we were going to church. They look and said yes she's definitely back. I cooked. Yes I cooked breakfast. They said what church are we going to. I said I don't know yet. Kira went to the calendar and began counting the Sundays. She said our church is having service. I said I really want to hear this other preacher. They said he is good. We dressed up. As we rode I looked at their faces. They were happy.

I was happy because this day I will rededicate myself to the Lord. I had come up thinking about what other people will say. Being ashamed of myself is one thing-but why should I care what people think or say. I guess that's why I didn't choose my church to go to that morning. I wanted to be among people who didn't know me. Who didn't judge me for my past.

I went to my cousin's church. The Pastor said something: you need to stop running-the only way you can fear sin is to look him dead in the eye. You got to stop running. God will be standing over it when it backs down-but you got to want sin to back down.

Reverend Sherman preached a motivational sermon, a sermon that I needed. As usual he called anyone to the altar who needed prayer. I was again ashamed. I felt warm. I could feel water running between my breasts. I could hear this little voice-it said okay, if you do this there is no turning back. It said are you sure-what if he changed his mind and appeared on your doorstep-you know you are not going to turn him down with his good looking self. That's when I realized that what I was in love with was his good looks, because other than that he was no better than any other man. Then I thought I wasn't ashamed when I was screwing him every time I got a chance. I prepared myself to go up to the altar. Kira said where you going mommy. I said to the altar. I stood up. Again, I wondered is this really what I want to do. I was standing there-I thought I could go to the bathroom but no this is something I got to do for me and my family. I knew this was the right thing to do. But I was so nervous.

When I arrived at the altar, the usher led me to a chair. My cousin came and stood behind me. Reverend Sherman asked me why I had come. I said for prayer and I want to rededicate myself to the Lord because I had lived in sin. There-I said it. The usher looked at me as if what kind of sin. Reverend Sherman said that was all he needed to know. He prayed with me and told me if I need counseling to give his missionary department for young women a call.

I felt good. A weight had been lifted off of my shoulders. I was able to admit it out loud.

# Chapter 35

I was doing well, things were looking up, but I have not faced my sins yet. Tuesday I was going through some things in my mind that connected us. I took a chance and called him. Yes I called the house. He answered. He told me that he would call me back. Well I left home to take care of something. Just as I walked in he called. We talked a few minutes-I told him I had a few things I had to get off my chest.

I told him that I thanked him for dumping me that everything was good, and I was doing fine. I didn't want to brag. I let him know that I missed him but I didn't want to see him. He may have thought I was pretending. But I wasn't pretending. God started opening doors for the kids and me. I started setting goals. I wanted to state in this phone call, it was the best thing to let you go. But instead I said take care of your kids, they are gonna need you. I had closure. But my biggest downfall was the things that I used to do like reading Psalm 25-I had stopped doing it. Once the doors started opening up I quickly forgot He had opened the doors for me. I began reading it again.

The next Wednesday night he showed up on the highway. He knows I'm speeding to work. So he goes the speed limit and sometimes slower. I could not pass him due to the curves. I tried to slow up so he could go on ahead but he slowed up too. I was smiling and laughing to myself. I wanted to stop him and ask him why he was fucking with me. My pride would not let me. But my heart and hormones said stop him. After battling with myself, I did it. I flashed my lights just before I turned off. He slowed up and hit his brakes-he went up and stopped and backed into this driveway. I thought he was going to come back. He just sat there. I kept driving to work. I passed the test. I just needed to keep reminding myself of the past. I did not want to revisit the past but doing it made me grow stronger.

## Chapter 36

The last visit with faith brought me over. The flesh is so weak but the spirit is strong. But there were 4 signs God gave me to let me know sin has lost. My 4 offspring. They love me no matter what. I need to be right for them and myself. I apologized to them for the last year for putting them 2nd. From now on they will be second only to the Lord.

A month later it was Christmas Eve. Michael stopped by unannounced. We talked on the porch. He did not deserve to come in my house. He tried to bring up old memories. I asked if we could have done it all over again what would you have done differently. He said never let you go. I said just like I figured. I turned and walked in the house and left him standing there.

Yes, I still love him-somehow I still want him-I will miss him-but when he is able to love me with the Lord only then can he have me. That goes for any man.

Some how I haven't let go but I must move on for the sake of my soul.

The Flesh is weak, not the spirit. Just say no to the flesh.

So is this you?

I know what you are saying-she should have left him a long time ago. Better yet, what did she ever see in him? My people can always judge, try to keep someone down and always remember the bad things about someone. They even try to tell you I would not have done that. But, they are the biggest hypocrites. Who are My People? It could be someone who is white, black, Hispanic or even Chinese. It could be male or female. Just don't let it be you.

So let us keep it real. Have you been in a bad relationship that you could not or did not want to let go?

# Chocolate Prince

It was 3:00 a.m. I was lying in my bed. I could not find sleep. Michael was on my mind. It has been 6 months. As I stare in the darkness, Luther Vandross was playing on the music channel on TV. You know the song "Superstar". This particular version had the pianist solo by Nat Adderly Jr. It was the live rendition.

As I listen, I can feel the tears come to my eyes and my chest tighten up. I asked in my mind why does this still hurt so badly? Why didn't Michael and I make it? As Nat Adderly begins to play his solo version, a tear rolled down my face. I was losing the fight to cry again. Usually I will say the Lord's Prayer to give me peace. I would lie in the bed many nights, close my eyes and repeat the Lord's Prayer.

Then the phone rang. He asked what are you doing. I say thinking about you. He says yeah. I say yes I need you to hold me. He said you know I'm just getting off work. I said I know. He said I need to hold you too. I said, I can wait to see you the kids are home. He said Yeah. I say thank you. He says for what? I don't know. He said good night sweetie. I then say good night to my new found friend Kevin.

Then I hear Luther say I don't want to be a fool for you .... I'm a fool for you.

I turn the TV off and said, I am a fool for the Lord. I said my prayers.

# *Discussion Questions*

1. How many women get involved with a man whether he is single or married and placed him before our children?
2. Why she was so hard headed?
3. Is it an old cliché that we will try something one time knowing that it is wrong.?
4. What part in the relationship did she not want to lose with Micheal Howard?
5. Were the effects that Darius Howard had on her was an excuse?
6. Did you see selfishness of Micheal when she begins to pay more attention to her children?
7. How many of you judge her and said what was wrong with her?
8. How many of you have been in a relationship that you could not let go.

# ACKNOWLEDGEMENTS

I could not have done this without the Lord, Jesus Christ, the Father, The Son and the Holy Ghost. You all are first in my life, YES I AM YOUR CHILD.

I would like to show appreciation to the following churches that have given me spiritual guidance; Pine Grove AME Church, Donovan Ga.; Buckeye Baptist Church, East Dublin, Ga.; Williams Chapel Baptist Church, Dublin Ga.; Tarvers Grove Baptist Church, Bartow, Ga.; Mt. Patmos Full Faith Gospel Church, Candler Rd. Decatur, GA.

To: Ashley, Brian, and Janique: let this be another lesson to learn. No matter what, don't let fears, rejection, denial, what someone may think of you and/or even say about you stop you. If you ever have a dream, idea or goal-don't let anything stop you. It took me all of my life to get over the fear. Don't let it take you this long. I know now only you can stop yourself. Nite Nite I love you.

To: My Mommy, Melzie Williams-for 81 years you have survived all kinds of storms-you have stood strong though it all and that strength has made me the woman I am today-I love you.

To: My father, brother, uncle and friend-I hope you are proud of me.

To: My Aunts Susie Wheeler and Jennette Wooten-thank you for being there through all the hard times and giving me the opportunity to know the Fann side of me.

To: Ms. Deanna Cooley and Mike Bright (PurePotential)-thank you for all the hugs and being patient with me over the last two years and encouraging me to finish.

To: Harlie Fulford Library, Wrightsville, GA., and Laurens Co. Memorial Library, Dublin, Ga.-Thank you for allowing me to use your facilities since I did not have a computer of my own.

To: Latasha Harrell (Dazzlin Doo's of Dublin GA.), my sister in Christ and one of my best friends-Thanks for making me beautiful and the last ten years of encouragement. Oh, thanks for listening.

To: Keith "Preacher" Brown-Thanks for saying "just because you come from a small town-don't mean you have to have a small town mentality".

To: My Aunt, Gloria May-It is between you and me what you did-thank you.

To: All my best friends Mary Taylor(my inspiration), Priscilla Brown, Robin Horne, Crystal Baker, Gwen Ammons (I missed you), Cynthia C.J. Johnson, Hazel Stephen, Latasha Harrell, Tracey Lemon, Tywanna Wright-Scott (my ace), Tammy Newton, Courtney Thomas and Sylvester Burton (stop smiling)-yes, I will not forget where I come from.

# ABOUT THE AUTHOR

She is the mother of 3 children: Ashley, Anthony (Brian), and Janique (NeNe). She is a graduate of Johnson County High School of Wrightsville GA. and Heart of Georgia Technical College of Dublin, GA. She was a member of Phi Beta Lambda. She was born, raised in and resides in Wrightsville, GA. She is affiliated with Pine Grove AME Church in Donovan, GA.

# Mail Order Form

Can't Let Go Part One: The Trial and Tribulation (18.95)

Shipping & Handling ($5.00)

Name:_____

Address:_____

City_____ State_____ Zip code:_____

Send checks or money orders to:

C C Fann
JABS Publications LLC
P O Box 81
Wrightsville, GA 31096

478-278-7956

Please allow 2-3 weeks for delivery.

# Purchase other items from CC Fann

## Common Sense Do Not Play The Game With An Inmate

## Can't Let Go Part One: The trial and Tribulation
## The Testimonial

## Can't Let Go Part Two the Hidden Agenda